HOLINESS
101

exploring this
transforming journey

Beacon Hill Press of Kansas City
Kansas City, Missouri

Library of Congress Cataloging-in-Publication Data

Holiness 101 : exploring this transforming journey.
    p. cm.
   ISBN 0-8341-2040-2
   1. Holiness—Church of the Nazarene. 2. Church of the Nazarene—Doctrines. I. Title: Holiness one hundred and one. II. Title: Holiness one hundred one. III. Beacon Hill Press of Kansas City (Kansas City, Mo.)
   BT767.H713 2003
   234'.8—dc21

                                                      2003001662

CONTENTS

PREFACE

Welcome to *Holiness 101*. And welcome to the adventure of exploring the transforming journey of Christian holiness. Your instructors/guides through this "course" have a passion for their subject. Their writings are designed to help you cut to the chase of this biblical theme in language that connects with life in the 21st century.

The first section of this primer will assist you in looking at a number of biblical truths and life experiences that form the warp and woof of Christian holiness. The second section offers insights, counsel, and inspiration for passing the vitality and hope of this life-changing experience to the next generation.

Most of these essays first appeared as articles in *Holiness Today*. This magazine is the primary voice in print of the Church of the Nazarene, serving English-speaking Nazarenes around the world and all Christians seeking holiness material. Articles in the monthly publication are written by pastors, lay experts in various fields of study, and denominational leaders. Subscriptions are available through Nazarene Publishing House.

You may want a copy of *Holiness 101* by your favorite chair in the den, on a nightstand, or within reach of where you sip your morning coffee. You'll find its message refreshing, compelling, and inspiring. And you'll likely want to refer to several of its articles again and again.

Ready for the quest? Peruse the text, meditate on each reading, and open your heart to the Spirit of holiness. You'll delight in the joys of discovery all along this transforming journey.

HOLINESS
core issues past and present

I WOULD LIKE GARDENING, IF IT WEREN'T FOR THE DIRT

randall e. davey

on a humid saturday morning nearly a decade ago, I reluctantly accepted an invitation to join old friends on a midday tour of the 1,050-acre Longwood Gardens in Kennett Square, Pennsylvania. Declining my offer to meet mid-point at an air-conditioned Denny's for extra crispy bacon and eggs scrambled, they countered with a guarantee. "You've never seen anything like it," they said. "It was the brainchild of Pierre Samuel Du Pont of the famous Du Ponts. William Penn owned the land before they did!"

It mattered little to me whose brainchild it was and to whom the land was originally deeded. Dirt was dirt, flowers were flowers, and that said it all for me. They met my silence with protests and a final compelling argument. "Come on. Longwood Gardens is one of the most formidable gardens in the world, and it's loaded with lighted fountains, sculptured bushes, ornate trees, a huge conservatory, waterfalls, statuary, and flora and fauna from all over the world. You've got to see it."

Frankly, it sounded like the kind of place I'd rather read about while fighting insomnia, but I masked my true sentiments and agreed to meet them at the appointed hour, under the condition that we do the culturally correct thing and "take tea at two."

I had no more than greeted my friends, paid the hefty admission price, and taken one glance when I immediately concluded, "The decision to come was a good move on my part." I couldn't believe it. Everywhere I looked, I saw manicured lawns, gorgeous roses, rippling brooks, and graveled walkways canopied by trees. Happy was I to forfeit Denny's Grand Slam for this feast. The buffet of floral loveliness seemed endless. By teatime, I was intoxicated with beauty.

My friends were so right. I couldn't have imagined it. Their pretour testimony was insufficient. No brochures rich with pictures could do it justice, and a library full of well-written articles would be only a rank substitute for seeing, smelling, and feeling the fragrance of God. I bid my friends adieu and drove home to the church manse with formal gardens on my mind.

I pulled up to the 1844 vintage farmhouse, replete with 20th-century additions, and envisioned things not as they were but as they could be. Without changing gear, I walked like a prophet on a mission to the backyard, unleashed the tangled hose hanging ingloriously from a rusty spigot, turned the water on full tilt, and put my thumb over the end of the hose to replicate Du Pont's fountains. I drenched a lone holly bush as I imagined a formal garden in my own backyard that would make Buckingham Palace pale in comparison. For a moment, I didn't even notice the field of mixed greens, weeds, and stubble—my "lawn."

I imagined a formal garden in my own backyard that would make Buckingham Palace pale in comparison.

It was 19-year-old Du Pont's brush with the illuminated fountains of the Champ de Mars, adjacent to the Eiffel Tower, that whet his re-creative passion. Pierre could not have known what he would spark in me, at age 43, during the summer of my discontent. Admittedly, Du Pont had a few francs on me and an extra 1,030 acres to work with, but I was undeterred. I was bent on converting the 20-acre parcel owned by Fairview Village Church of the Nazarene into "The Village Gardens of Fairview." I could see it clearly. I pictured fami-

lies strolling together on a Sunday afternoon,
bathing in the beauty of our campus.

With shovel in tow, I muscled my way from
dreams to reality. Friends helped me haul native
rock to the backyard while others hauled in
truckloads of dirt. My creativity reached an all-
time high as my companions and I built a verita-
ble fortress in the backyard. The project took on a
life of its own and grew in proportion daily. I
imagined English ivy cascading over the stone
walls and a variety of flowers and shrubs accent-
ing the house.

About four weeks into the project, my backyard looked anything but scenic. Piles of dirt and
rock were as high as my passion for the project
was low. It was already dawning on me, up to my
knees in clay soil, that there was a substantive
gap between my dream and the formidable reality. On that hot August afternoon, I concluded that
I would really like gardening if it weren't for the
dirt.

Nine years later, my backyard, though show-
ing progress, is still not quite ready for tours. In
fact, our "upper pond" fell prey to the summer
drought. Where ducks swam last spring, we have
enough dry grass to bale hay. My attempt at
sculpting bushes went south along with my
wrong-time-of-the-season tree pruning. There's
some question about whether the cherry tree in
the "north 40" will survive at all. At this writing,
my statuary is limited to one concrete bench

standing solo west of the circular herb garden and a lone birdbath at its center. The only evidence that the mound of growth actually is an herb garden is a sign swearing that it's so.

I can't say much for my David Austin roses either. Two of them look more like an exhibit for fungus, overzealous bugs, and mutant strains of killer vines. The third has been whacked two seasons in a row by the snowplow, and only one stem with one blossom survived the back-to-back assaults. My butterfly bushes are out of control as well. On a windy day, they resemble King Kong engulfing the Empire State Building.

I'm the only one who knows that the piles of upended sod are flower beds in the making. In short, I have no plans to approach the Fairview Village church board with a suggestion to change the name to "The Village Gardens of Fairview." Not yet, anyhow.

Though I no longer trumpet my dream aloud, I still occasionally stand in the backyard of the manse and imagine what it could be. I still see pools of clear water, an impressive geyser at each center. I see sculpted bushes, tall trees, prize-winning roses, and a verdant, manicured lawn. I know it's possible because I've seen Du Pont's Longwood dream come true.

Come to think of it, all of us are garden people. We root to an idyllic nursery the likes of which no Du Pont could ever replicate and no brochure, picture, or testimony could ever describe. There, Adam and Eve, though shaded by fruited trees, traded conversation with God in the cool of the day for talk-lite, eggs scrambled, coffee black, and thorns and thistles. Humankind has trudged in conflict from dust to dust ever since, existing by the sweat of the brow, wandering like sheep without a Shepherd, trying to rediscover Eden.

Not by man's own choosing but by God's gracious doing, the way back to the future was revealed through the Word become flesh. Followers of the Living Word pilgrim with Him on a holy pathway, a way poetically outlined in the written Word, an enduring road map from here to there. It is the pathway of holiness, scenic but narrow.

The people called Nazarenes see things and folks not as they are but as they can be. They look at the thorns and thistles of humanity and see rich possibilities, new creations, transformed minds, and pure hearts.

There is no brochure or picture that does justice to the Redeemer and Sanctifier.

Nazarenes don't deny reality; they recognize humankind's plight. They admit that as our common lot, we were born with a penchant to sin and we have. They recognize that we contend with God and would be God, at least of our own existence. Nazarenes realize that we can work in our spiritual garden for a lifetime and never achieve God's dream. We can't negotiate with God. We can't buy our way in or earn heaven credits by trying harder and doing more. We can only confess our need for a Savior and the transforming filling of His Holy Spirit.

Those who have received the grace of the triune God testify to it. They say to the unbelieving, "You won't believe it. You've got to experience it." Yet testimonies aren't sufficient. There is no brochure or picture that does justice to the Redeemer and Sanctifier. An empty cross where the blood of Jesus was shed remains for many a holiday symbol or good luck charm and nothing more.

To the unbelieving around the world, Nazarenes are compelled to say, "Come. You must walk through the garden with our Host. Come, experience a people marked by compassion, kindness, humility, gentleness, and patience. Come, be part of a grace-based fellowship of forgiving, loving people, imitators of Christ. Come. Come to the Christ of God who is central to our conversation, He who invites us in and makes possible audience with the Holy One. He's the One who chooses us and calls us and makes those who repent whiter than snow. He will help us seek out the 'Holy, holy, holy, Lord God Almighty!' His Spirit empowers us to imitate the Christ of history, who is the Christ of the present and the Christ of the future."

Sound idyllic? Do you take exception to the notion that God wills people to be like Him . . . to be holy? While we walk through our imperfect congregational gardens of mixed greens, weeds,

and stubble, admittedly we witness strife, jealousy, anger, disputes, dissensions, factions, envy,
and impurity. Singly and collectively, they are
lethal. But we remain optimistic.

Though we Nazarenes stand in clay soil up to
our knees and taste Adamic dust in our mouths,
we remain confident that God wills our sanctification, our spiritual wholeness, our personal and
congregational holiness, and we believe that His
grace in response to our faith makes it possible.

So come. Walk in holy gardens, whose builder
and maker is God. In this book, other writers will
spell out more clearly our biblical understandings
of the tremendous mystery called holiness. Join
us on the journey.

Randall E. Davey is senior pastor of Seattle Aurora Church of the
Nazarene. This article was first published in *Holiness Today*,
April 2002.

HOLINESS 101

wesley d. tracy

God alone is intrinsically holy. This does not mean merely that His moral standards are higher than ours. The Creator is different and distinct from the creation. God is beyond us, alone inhabiting the category of "the holy."

Therefore, all human holiness is derived from God's. Holiness is not something we can earn like a wage, produce by meticulous ritual, or concoct from a recipe like taffy. Holiness is a gift of God bestowed upon the heart of the fully surrendered believer.

Human history began in the Garden of Eden, where humankind was created in God's image. But our first parents sinned away their pure relationship with a holy God. Since then the human record is one of sinful self-centeredness. The new beginning for the human race bloomed in the garden of the Resurrection, when Jesus Christ, the Lamb of God, defeated our great enemies: sin and death.

God spoke His holiness and His love in a human metaphor—Jesus, the Son of God. Through His Son and His Spirit, God calls us back to holiness.

God spoke His holiness and His love in a human metaphor—Jesus, the Son of God.

For centuries, Christians have experienced God's redeeming grace in two dimensions. The first dimension is saving grace, what we often call that act of God in which we are born again. The Nazarene Articles of Faith use such terms as *justification, adoption,* and *regeneration* to describe our common experience.

The second dimension of redemption, *sanctifying grace,* occurs after the born-again experience. God's people have experienced sanctifying grace in two aspects. Usually a conscious *transforming moment* is experienced in which the consecrated heart is purified by faith and filled with the Spirit. This moment is a gateway to the deeper life of holiness, the *transforming journey* described in 2 Corinthians 3:18. Early Nazarenes testified to both aspects of holiness by saying, "I am sanctified, and I am being sanctified."

A primary mission of the Wesleyan-Holiness people is to help believers find that deeper life of holiness. Sometimes we call it our cardinal doctrine.

Wesley D. Tracy is an author, speaker, and preacher in the Church of the Nazarene. This article was first published in *Holiness Today,* April 2002.

Our Story Tells Us Who We Are

dan boone

tucking a child into bed is a formative event, so for each of my daughters I created a bedtime story—the Amy story, the Ashley story, and the Abby story. Each story included their loving family, their naming, their behavior, our hopes. I wanted my daughters to know who they are.

Deep in every human heart is a desire to know the purpose of life. We want to know to whom we belong and who belongs to us. We want a clear "ought" to inform our choices. We want to know where we've been and where we're going. We want to know who we are.

Lacking this, we wander aimlessly. We fight to secure our place. We compete to prove our worth. We use or are used.

This need not be. We have a story, an old story. It has an ending, which is more a beginning. For those who belong to God, the story might be told like this:

We were slaves. Brickmaking defined our existence. Collect straw. Tramp it in mud pits. Pour it into forms. Let it dry. Build Pharaoh's empire. Then Moses announced that God had heard our cries and was moving to liberate us. Pharaoh first responded to Moses' demands by raising the daily brick quota. But 10 plagues later, he told us to get out. We remember that dark night, that meal of lamb, bitter herbs, and unleavened bread. We ate hurriedly, dressed to travel. While we waited inside, God moved outside. Egypt's hold on us loosened as breath left her every firstborn. Our future no longer belonged to Pharaoh but to God. We walked beneath blood-smeared doorposts into freedom. But freedom for what? We would soon find out.

Months later we stood at the foot of a smoking mountain. Moses announced God's vision for us. "If you obey my voice and keep my covenant, you shall be my treasured possession out of all the peoples. Indeed, the whole earth is mine, but you shall be for me a priestly kingdom and a holy nation" (Exodus

19:5-6, NRSV). "You shall be holy, for I the LORD your God am holy" (Leviticus 19:2, NRSV). Next came the Ten Commandments, God's vision statement for creation. In the first four, God described our relationship with Him: unquestioned loyalty, undivided worship, uncompromised obedience. In the next six, God called us to treat each other with respect and care and to extend the same to strangers, to property, and to animals and the earth. Being a holy people meant right relationship with God, others, and the world.

These two events—the midnight liberation and the gift of the Law—changed everything. We understood what our lives were to mean. We were no longer slaves to Pharaoh's old ways. We were free children of God, liberated for worship and service. We would walk into a future we could never have imagined, guided by God's law.

But we proved our fickleness. Our story is saddened with words all too descriptive of our response to God. "Stiff-necked." "Hard-hearted." "Did what was right in their own eyes." At times, God's anger blazed. But He refused to give up on us. God loves stubbornly. So new promises were made.

"The days are surely coming, says the LORD, when I will make a new covenant with the house of Israel and the house of Judah. It will not be like the covenant that I made with

their ancestors when I took them by the hand
to bring them out of the land of Egypt—a covenant that they broke. . . . But this is the covenant that I will make with the house of
Israel after those days, says the LORD: I
will put my law within them, and I will
write it on their hearts; and I will be
their God, and they shall be my people"
(Jeremiah 31:31-33, NRSV). "A new heart
I will give you, and a new spirit I will
put within you; and I will remove from
your body the heart of stone and give
you a heart of flesh. I will put my
[S]pirit within you, and make you follow my statutes and be careful to ob-
serve my ordinances" (Ezekiel 36:26-27, NRSV).

Jesus became the flesh-and-blood vision statement of God.

These promises marked new possibilities.
We would be energized from within by the
breath of God. We would be empowered by
the Spirit to live God's vision. We would be
holy because the Source of our life is holy.

After a long time, God moved again. The
Spirit came upon Mary, and the Child she bore
was holy, God's Son. Filled with the Spirit, Jesus became the flesh-and-blood vision statement of God. Everything the Ten Commandments required, Jesus lived. Every promise in
the Law leaped to life in His words and deeds.
In Him, we saw holiness. His loyalty to the Father was unquestioned; His worship, undivided; His obedience, uncompromised. He treated

His brothers and sisters with respect and care. He moved mercifully toward the poor and the outcast. He viewed all creation a gift, from bread to fish to pungent perfume. "In him was life, and the life was the light of all people" (John 1:4, NRSV).

Jesus moved among us, liberating us from demons and disease, labels and legalism, death and destruction. Then, one dark afternoon, He died in our place. We stood once again under a blood-smeared post. He took our sin upon himself and went into every dark place we would ever be asked to go, even the pit of death. Then God raised Him from the dead, and 50 days later He poured the Holy Spirit on us. Holiness is possible because God gives us the Spirit of the risen Christ. We embrace each day as a new creation. We live as the sanctified, free children of God. Our hope is fueled by the promise of God: One day the lamb will lie down with the lion, peace will cover the earth, justice will flow like a mighty stream, and every knee shall bow and every tongue proclaim that Jesus is Lord!

This is our story. It tells us the purpose of life. We know who and whose we are. We embrace tomorrow with faith because God calls us to be His holy people and makes it possible by His Spirit.

The Church of the Nazarene celebrates this grand story. We are former slaves. We are children of blood-smeared doorposts. We are people of the visionary law. We are recipients of new hearts. We are heirs with the resurrected Jesus. We are the Body of Christ, the Church empowered by the Spirit of God. And we are radically optimistic about our future.

This optimism finds expression in the Wesleyan-Holiness message of entire sanctification. We believe that God's liberating activity—justification, adoption, regeneration—finds its earthly expression in our sanctification. We have words for this "holy-making activity" of God:

Perfection. By this, we mean that God has a vision for our lives. By His Spirit, He is patterning us after Christ. We are becoming what God intends us to be.

Entire sanctification. This phrase bespeaks a necessary moment. The passing of time does not automatically ensure holiness. Our story demonstrates our capacity for stiff-necked, Egypt-loving, fickle hearts. We would wander aimlessly. The experience of fellow travelers reveals a decisive moment when God does something inward, and the Bible defines this activity with decisive words —*cleansed, purified, dead to sin, alive to God, unified with Him in death, slaves to righteousness.* Article X of the *Manual of the Church of the Nazarene* describes it like this:

> We believe that entire sanctification is that act of God, subsequent to regeneration, by which believers are made free from original sin, or depravity, and brought into a state of

entire devotement to God, and the holy obedience of love made perfect.

It is wrought by the baptism with the Holy Spirit, and comprehends in one experience the cleansing of the heart from sin and the abiding, indwelling presence of the Holy Spirit, empowering the believer for life and service.

Entire sanctification is provided by the blood of Jesus, is wrought instantaneously by faith, preceded by entire consecration; and to this work and state of grace the Holy Spirit bears witness.

Love. We speak of love or perfect love. John Wesley defined entire sanctification as love expelling all sin. God being love, to be filled with the Spirit of God is to be filled with love. This love is not sentimentalism; it is the love expressed in the Ten Commandments and embodied in the person of Jesus. It is love with backbone. It is merciful and compassionate, loyal to God, respectful of humans, careful with creation.

God's vision for our lives is conformity to His Son.

Christlikeness. The world may wrestle with other definitions, but likeness to Jesus Christ is a clear, compelling call. God's vision for our lives is conformity to His Son. We are made Christlike by the sanctifying work of His Spirit.

We may use other terms—*pure heart, single eye, Spirit-filled, fullness of the blessing.* All reflect our optimism that God has liberated us from sin to make us His holy servants, His treasured possession, the people of Jesus.

As we embraced God's call to holiness, we sometimes failed. Our story as Nazarenes includes times when we were more concerned with how we "looked" to the world than with "seeing" the world as God sees it. We often have interpreted God's law as a narrow, individualistic guide to sainthood when it was meant to create a new community. We sometimes thought of sanctification as a private experience when God meant to sanctify us into a Spirit-shaped community. We sometimes made this second moment of grace the goal of our experience rather than the gate to wholehearted service to God and others.

When we refuse to identify ourselves as "sinners," we are not being arrogant. We believe that holy people should be quick to confess sin. But in the story that identifies us, we are addressed not as "sinners of God" but as "saints of God." God's vision statement tells us that we are a treasured possession, a Spirit-filled people, the Body of Christ, and saints, which means "holy ones." Our story tells us who we are.

Dan Boone is pastor of College Church of the Nazarene, Bourbonnais, Illinois, and a member of the teaching faculty at Nazarene Theological Seminary in Kansas City. He and his wife, Denise, have three children. This article was first published in *Holiness Today*, April 2002.

Our Shared Story

wesley d. tracy

nazarenes are deeply rooted in biblical faith. We affirm the sufficiency of the Old Testament and New Testament to reveal God's will "concerning us in all things necessary to our salvation" (*Manual,* paragraph 4). Our faith in the Bible goes far beyond intellectual assent. It is a profound conviction that therein lies the eternal truth that shapes our souls, molds our worldview, and stirs our imagination to visions of the glory of God. Nazarenes declare, "Whatever is not contained [in the Bible] is not to be enjoined as an article of faith" (*Manual,* paragraph 4).

Our family history shows that we are distinctly Christian. God makes himself known most clearly in Jesus Christ, whose incarnation, crucifixion, and resurrection reveal God's love and reconcile sinners. Christ is the Second Person of the Holy Trinity and the true Savior.

We also are part of the Protestant story. "Protesting" doesn't top our priority list. Rather, we embrace the principles that fueled the Protestant Reformation: salvation by grace alone, justification by faith alone, the Bible as the rule of faith and practice and the priesthood of all believers.

The flame of the Wesleyan revival of 18th-century England lights another chapter in our story. Just as the Protestant Reformation rediscovered *justification* by faith, the Wesleyan revival rediscovered *sanctification* by faith. Nazarenes endorse the core values of the Wesleyan movement:

Mutual spiritual guidance

A commitment to the poor

Holiness of both heart and life

Our family saga includes the Holiness Movement that swept 19th-century America. Our ecclesiastical ancestors were eager participants in this movement, which flowed across denominational lines to create a fellowship of those baptized by the sanctifying Spirit.

Deeply rooted in a heritage worth treasuring, yet earnest about being relevant to our own age, we face the sunrise of the 21st century with optimism, ready to follow the Spirit and to write new stories of worship, evangelism, nurture, and service.

This article was first published in *Holiness Today*, April 2002.

ENTIRE SANCTIFICATION: NO APOLOGIES

philip r. hamner

it is a conversation I have heard many times before. "Who are the Nazarenes? What do they believe?" It is the answer that draws my earnest attention, though, because the response of my fellow Nazarenes to the question of our identity is so varied that at times I wonder who we are. Usually the answer includes some attempt to point out the Nazarene commitment to holy living. Often there is a brief and basic explanation of how God can make us holy, but in almost every instance, Nazarenes sound all too apologetic about what we believe.

I am left wondering why we are so "afraid" of the doctrine of holiness. Why are we hesitant to talk about it? It appears as if we think it is a "funny" notion that only Nazarenes believe. One who receives such an apologetic explanation of what Nazarenes believe can only surmise that holiness or sanctification, as we understand it, is something weird. It must be a quirky add-on to our faith.

Nothing could be further from the truth. The Nazarene understanding of holiness stands firmly on the ground of Holy Scripture. Our commitment to the doctrine of sanctification flows out of the very character and nature of God. That which we confess as our faith rests solidly within the norm of Christian tradition. We should not be ashamed. In fact, we should be excited about our calling to spread scriptural holiness throughout the land. So how do we demonstrate in our witness that holiness is central to what our Lord did for us in His death and resurrection?

holiness at the heart of the old testament

Immediately, from the very first pages of the Bible, we discover a God who intends to give himself to His creation. In the exchange of creation, we find God desiring above all else to have relationship with us. In response, we turned away and rejected Him. Suddenly, we were exposed to evil and separated from our Creator. We, who were created in His image, were now scarred by sin and left for dead. God did not leave us in our sin, however. He began the eternal work of restoring us to relationship with Him. In the process our Father also set out to heal the internal wounds of rebellion and disobedience.

He gave His children the Ten Commandments. The commandments were to be the way to live in this world. Supreme allegiance to the one true living God and utter devotion to the needs of one's neighbors are the essential nature of these commands. God insisted that His children live by these relationship principles, declaring, "For I am the LORD who brought you up from the land of Egypt, to be your God; you shall be holy, for I am holy" (Lev. 11:45, NRSV).

God does not call us to self-cleansing; it is from first to last the work of God in us.

We see, then, that the very essence of God's offer of salvation is in making us like Him. Holiness and righteousness mark His call, and like Him we shall be. Yet it is love that stands at the center of God's offer of salvation. First, we are to love the Lord our God completely (Deut. 6:4-6). Second, we are to love our neighbors as ourselves (Lev. 19:18). To be like God is to love others unconditionally.

Up to this point we might be concerned that the demands of holiness are unbearable. We might also assert that the demands are unreasonable, because *we* cannot achieve them in our lifetime. Our concerns undoubtedly would be valid, *except* that *God* intends to do this work in us. The Nazarene doctrine of holiness is not a doctrine of self-purification; God does not call us to self-cleansing. The demands of God in the Law drive us to our knees. We cannot live this life in our own strength. It is from first to last the work of God in us that makes us holy.

So, if we will keep reading our Bibles, we will discover God's desire to transform us. That's the message of the prophets. Both Jeremiah and Ezekiel speak of God's desire to fix the problem we have created. Jeremiah speaks in terms of the Law being fulfilled in us when he says, "I will put my law within them, and I will write it on their hearts; and I will be their God, and they shall be my people. No longer shall they teach one another, or say to each other, 'Know the LORD,' for they shall all know me, from the least of them to the greatest, says the LORD; for I will forgive their iniquity, and remember their sin no more" (Jer. 31:33-34, NRSV).

Nothing less than a real transformation stands at the center of God's very purposes for us.

It's not enough simply to wipe the slate of sin clean from our lives. God desires to give us the internal power to follow Him. A new heart and a new spirit to love and serve God and this world is His eternal pledge (Ezek. 36:26). Nothing less than a real transformation stands at the center of God's very purposes for us. Who will bring this glorious promise to life in us? He is Jesus, the Christ.

Jesus Christ: the promise of full redemption

So here we are at the center of our faith. Jesus Christ is our salvation. God has promised to bring deliverance from willful sin in this lifetime. Since we cannot master such a feat for ourselves, we must turn to the fulfillment of it in Jesus Christ. Indeed, Christ has fulfilled the promise of full redemption. When "the Word became flesh and lived among us" (John 1:14, NRSV), all the power of God was brought to bear on the human heart.

One important way that the Early Church spoke about the mission and purpose of Christ was this: He became what we are, so that we could become what He is. Sanctification is the work of God that makes us like Him. Sanctification encompasses the whole of the Christian experience. It begins in the new birth, when God makes us alive together with Him (Col. 2:13). Christ himself tells us that it is the pure in heart who will see God (Matt. 5:8). This is no "add-on" to the Christian faith. The call, command, and provision of holiness are the Christian faith. Christlikeness is not a point of human achievement, nor is it a place of boasting. To be like Christ is to be holy.

Still further, the work of God in sanctification has an instantaneous element to it. In the moment of our new birth in Christ, we are instantaneously brought from death to life. Following this, a deeper work of sanctification, entire sanctification, is to be received by the believer. In this work of God, the believer is cleansed from the inward disposition to rebellion. To testify to the importance of this work, the Holiness Movement of which our church is a part was brought into existence by the urging of the Holy Spirit.

A deeper work of cleansing is promised and provided by the blood of Christ.

It is true that at times our tradition has emphasized this instantaneous work to the exclusion of the gradual or progressive work of sanctification. However, the value of deliverance from sin in this lifetime cannot be underestimated. To this glorious hope the Scriptures testify over and over again. Entire sanctification is implied in the promises of Jeremiah 31 and Ezekiel 36. It is prayed for in Psalm 51. The apostles confirm the reality of entire sanctification by their own testimonies.

The apostle Paul leads each of his churches to discover that in God's great plan of salvation, a deeper work of cleansing is promised and provided by the blood of Christ. To the Roman church Paul writes, "But thanks be to God that you, having once been slaves of sin, have become obedient from the heart to the form of teaching to which you were entrusted, and that you, having been set free from sin, have become slaves of righteousness. . . . But now that you have been freed from sin and enslaved to God, the advantage you get is sanctification" (Rom. 6:17-18, 22, NRSV). For the Thessalonian church Paul prays, "May the God of peace himself sanctify you entirely; and may your spirit and soul and body be kept sound and blameless at the coming of our Lord Jesus Christ (1 Thess. 5:23, NRSV).

The other apostles were no less enthusiastic in urging the truth of entire sanctification to their flocks. The apostle John helps believers live in the power of the sanctifying grace of God when he writes, "If we walk in the light as he himself is in the light, we have fellowship with one another, and the blood of Jesus his Son cleanses us from all sin" (1 John 1:7, NRSV). The apostle Peter says of Christ's provision for holiness, "His divine power has given us everything needed for life and godliness, through the knowledge of him who called us by his own glory and goodness" (2 Peter 1:3, NRSV).

sanctification: the goal and purpose of the christian life

With this much biblical support for the doctrine of sanctification, why do we act as if we are embarrassed by the teaching? The reasons are probably many. We don't understand it. We haven't experienced entire sanctification. We don't want to sound boastful. Yet, something so central to the Christian faith should not be ignored. Sanctification does stand as the goal and purpose of the Christian life. We Nazarenes should celebrate our privilege in sharing God's promise of a clean heart with any and all who will hear it. Holiness is received by faith and is woven into nearly every page of the Scriptures.

The next time someone asks you what Nazarenes believe, go ahead; tell the truth. Tell the whole truth. Then, as the revelation of God's grace is unfurled, watch as God does His incredible work of renewal yet again.

Philip R. Hamner is pastor of the Overland Park, Kansas, Church of the Nazarene. He and his wife, Rebecca, are the parents of Evan Philip. This article was first published in *Holiness Today*, April 2002.

HOLINESS, OUR SACRED TRUST

wesley d. tracy

the nazarene doctrine of holiness is founded firmly in Scripture. That God is holy and calls us to be holy is pictured in the Pentateuch, sung in the Psalms, proclaimed in the Prophets, demonstrated in the Gospels, and explained in the Epistles.

The Old Testament word for God's holiness, *Qodesh,* has three levels of meaning. First, it means *separation.* "I am God and no mortal" (Hos. 11:9, NRSV). Second, it means the *glory* or burning splendor of God's presence. We could not bear that blazing glory in its fullness, so God accommodates our limitations through the Incarnation. Third, holiness means *purity.*

God loves us and accepts us just as we are. But He will not leave us just as we are. He wants to cleanse our hearts and fill us with the Holy Spirit so that we can be just like Jesus. The closer we draw to God, the greater will grow our thirst to be like Christ. Submerged longings to be free from every stain of sin will burst forth like tulips reaching for the sun.

Nazarene theologian H. Ray Dunning says sanctification provides: (1) freedom *for* God, (2) freedom *for* others, (3) freedom *from* the earth, and (4) freedom *from* self-domination.

God has given some churches special gifts for the benefit of the whole Body. Among them, the Church of the Nazarene has an important role to play. As long as the Lutherans are among us, we will never forget that salvation is by grace alone and not by works. As long as the Presbyterians are among us, we will never lose the doctrine of the sovereignty of God. As long as the Baptists are among us, we will never forget the authority of the Bible. And as long as the Nazarenes and other Holiness groups are among us, the family of churches will never forget that all believers are called to sanctification. We did not invent holiness, but God has given us a special responsibility for sharing it with the world.

This article was first published in *Holiness Today*, April 2002.

THE GRAND PLAN

h. david mckellips

and we, who with unveiled faces all reflect the Lord's glory, are being transformed into his likeness with ever-increasing glory, which comes from the Lord, who is the Spirit" (2 Cor. 3:18).

The magnitude of the plan still amazes me.

During the 1999 and 2000 football seasons, we who live in Oklahoma witnessed Coach Bob Stoops take a mediocre University of Oklahoma football team and turn it into a national champion. As remarkable as this was, and as excited as fans became, that feat pales in comparison to the incredible transformation the apostle Paul describes in his second letter to Corinth. The announcement is startling: God's grand plan is to transform people like me into the very likeness of Christ!

The work begins when one trusts in Christ and is born again. In the new birth, the Holy

Spirit actually takes up residence in a Christian and begins the process of bringing all of that person's life into conformity with Christ. God's grand plan is that we more and more will be like Christ in our thoughts, feelings, and actions. What an unbelievable adventure!

Unfortunately, the universal experience of Christians is that even after the new birth, all of life is not necessarily submitted to God's will. As the Holy Spirit reveals how thorough the claims of Christ and His kingdom are, He bumps into believers' stubborn desire to keep control of selected areas of life. While it is true that believers do welcome Christ into their lives, most have no idea at that time that they will have to die to controlling their own lives and futures.

In discipleship classes at my local church, I often use an old analogy to illustrate the full consecration required in the journey of the sanctified life. We often think of Jesus entering our lives as a guest. We invite Jesus in and want Him to have a place in the living room as we relish the gifts He brings—the freedom of His forgiveness and the joy of life with purpose and meaning. But we close other rooms of our lives to Him. For some, the room representing finances is off-limits to Christ's direction. Others shut the door to the room representing entertainments that do not match His holy presence. For others, the closed room may represent relationships, work, the past, or the future. But Christ is not content to remain a guest. The work of the Holy Spirit is to lead us to the place where we take Christ through the entire inner house of our lives and invite Him to become not a guest but owner and master. We turn the deed over to Him and ask Him to change anything in our lives that does not match His character or bring honor to His name.

"MY HEART,
CHRIST'S HOME"
book
video

In Romans 6:19, the apostle Paul calls believers to take this deliberate and decisive action: "Just as you used to offer the parts of your body in slavery to impurity and to ever-increasing wickedness, so now offer them in slavery to righteousness leading to holiness."

I love the way Al Truesdale and Bonnie Perry describe this transforming moment of entire sanctification: "To be wholly or entirely sanctified means that we place our whole existence at the disposal of the Kingdom. It involves the Holy Spirit cleansing us from any lingering obstruction to Christ's Lordship and empowering us for victorious living and service. The term sanctification communicates a point of departure as well as a destination. It means placing all of life in the stream of transforming grace" *(A Dangerous Hope)*.

Although entirely sanctified believers belong exclusively to God and are free from sinful self-domination, they have a great deal of growing to do! We need to be careful that we do not so emphasize the transforming moments of conversion and sanctification that we neglect the transforming journey that begins in these crisis experiences. The sanctified believer still suffers from the effects of sin on the body and mind, the scars from past sinful living, and a thousand faults that hinder God's purpose. But God's grand plan is in progress.

After the believer places all of life in the stream of transforming grace, growth is neither optional nor automatic. The apostle Paul urges us to "purify ourselves from everything that contaminates body and spirit, perfecting holiness out of reverence for God" (2 Cor. 7:1). He reminds the Ephesians that the goal is to "become mature, attaining to the whole measure of the fullness of Christ" (4:13).

After the believer places all of life in the stream of transforming grace, growth is neither optional nor automatic.

But how is God's transforming and renewing grace given to us? It comes through personal prayer and Bible study, fellowship and accountability with other Christians, daily fellowship with the Holy Spirit to ask His advice and then yield to it, and a heart that is open to the preached Word and the sacraments. These disciplines, or means of grace, are not ends in themselves, but they do create the conditions in which God's transforming grace may flow more freely.

At times I wish the transformation of my character could happen as quickly as the transformation of Oklahoma's football team. Nevertheless, I press on to reach the goal, the grand plan that Christ has laid before me, "being confident of this, that he who began a good work in [me] will carry it on to completion until the day of Christ Jesus" (Phil. 1:6).

H. David McKellips is senior pastor of Central Church of the Nazarene in Tulsa, Oklahoma. This article was first published in *Holiness Today*, April 2002.

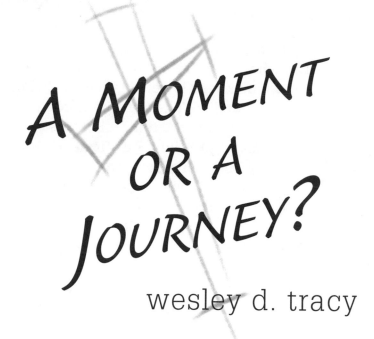

A MOMENT OR A JOURNEY?

wesley d. tracy

God's goal in sanctification is to enable believers to "love the Lord . . . with all your heart and with all your soul and with all your mind. . . . And . . . your neighbor as yourself" (Matt. 22:37; 39). God wants to drench us in love and set us apart for holy use.

But even though we are born-again believers, we may soon find something less than love inhabiting corners of the heart. Perhaps a part of the heart treasures lust, harbors a lurking self-idolatry, nourishes a cultural prejudice, shelters a smoldering resentment. These form the hyphenated sins of the spirit: self-sufficiency, self-love, self-righteousness, self-pity.

Picture a fortified castle: strong stone walls,

vigilant guards, a deep moat. Safe and secure,
right? But what if, in the still of night, an enemy
inside the castle keeps lowering the drawbridge
for the enemy outside? The not-yet-sanctified
heart can be like that. It betrays our
loftiest aspirations, our firmest resolu-
tions, and our best intentions.

Sanctification

is about

both the

transforming

moment and

a lifelong

transforming

journey into

wholeness

and holiness.

The hyphenated sins of the spirit re-
quire hyphenated acts of consecration:
self-surrender, self-denial, self-tran-
scendence, self-donation. Self-surrender does not mean self-annihilation.
There is a sinful self to be crucified
with Christ, a natural self to be disciplined in Christ, and a true self to be
actualized in Christ.

Consecration and sanctification are
not the same thing. Consecration is our
commitment and is a prelude to God's
act of sanctification. Sanctification is
about both the transforming moment
and a lifelong transforming journey into wholeness and holiness.

The transforming moment of sanctification
does not give us a lifetime supply of holiness. The
cleansing and filling work of the Spirit is a moment-by-moment experience that goes on in the
daily give-and-take of life. With Charles Wesley
we sing, "Every moment, Lord, I need the merit of
Thy death" (John Wesley, *Letters,* 4:208). The Spirit shows us our lacks and lapses and cultivates

spiritual sensitivities of which we were unaware when we first prayed the sinner's prayer.

The deepest peace we will ever know, the most satisfying fulfillment we will ever experience, and the most throw-our-hats-in-the-air joy we will ever celebrate all lie on the far side of loving submission to the sanctifying Spirit. It's a moment . . . *and* a journey.

This article was first published in *Holiness Today*, April 2002.

HOLY AND HIS

frank moore

May God himself, the God of peace, sanctify you through and through. May your whole spirit, soul and body be kept blameless at the coming of our Lord Jesus Christ. The one who calls you is faithful and he will do it (1 Thess. 5:23-24).

I urge you, brothers, in view of God's mercy, to offer your bodies as living sacrifices, holy and pleasing to God—this is your spiritual act of worship. Do not conform any longer to the pattern of this world, but be transformed by the renewing of your mind. Then you will be able to test and approve what God's will is—his good, pleasing and perfect will (Rom. 12:1-2).

Jesus spoke often about being totally sold out to God. He said becoming a Christian is like selling all you have and taking the money to buy a valuable pearl. Or it's like taking all your money to buy a piece of property that has buried treasure on it. Jesus told the rich young ruler that he needed to sell his possessions and follow Him. Jesus did not oppose owning possessions, but He was opposed to them becoming our gods. Being the person God wants us to be requires a total sell-out.

thinking about the truth in everyday language

The Christian journey begins the moment we ask Christ into our lives. It continues until we go to be with the Lord forever. As we grow and develop in our faith, God opens new doors of commitment through which we walk. Entire sanctification is one of those doors.

The Bible often speaks of sanctification, which basically means the total, lifelong process of becoming holy. Because the process begins with the new birth, we call the spiritual growth immediately following regeneration "initial sanctification." That is, we begin walking God's way. The fruit of the Spirit in our lives becomes evidence that a change has taken place.

The process of spiritual growth may continue for months or even years before we sense a need for something more in our Christian journey. The common experience of saints down through the ages has been an awareness of a remaining hindrance to further spiritual progress. No outward sin—just an uncertain gnawing for something more. This awareness usually takes the form of an internal battle with the self, such as Paul described in Gal. 5:16-26. In summary he said, "The sinful nature desires what is contrary to the Spirit, and the Spirit what is contrary to the sinful nature. They are in conflict with each other, so that you do not do what you want" (v. 17).

The battle may be self-centeredness in the form of self-seeking, self-assertion, self-indulgence, self-sufficiency, or self-will—all as a preference over God or others. It's not that we don't wish to please God—we do. Our problem involves wanting the best of both worlds: having what God wants *and* what we want at the same time. We realize we cannot have it both ways. We have been plagued with this problem since the Fall in the Garden of Eden.

> *Once we pinpoint the self-centeredness, we realize it must be replaced with Christ-centeredness.*

Once we pinpoint the self-centeredness, we realize it must be replaced with Christ-centeredness. We confess our need to God and surrender ourselves completely to His will. The old-timers called it "dying out to self." They did not mean self-extinction or psychological suicide; rather, they meant self-preference replaced with God-preference. After full surrender comes faith in God to change us. We trust God to accept our consecration and fill us completely with His Holy

Spirit. The Spirit entered our life when we accepted Christ; now we are inviting Him to take charge of our control center.

Entire sanctification is God's gift. We do not earn or deserve it any more than we earned or deserved regeneration. We consecrate; God sanctifies. So the two experiences of grace are similar in that we ask in faith, and God grants us His gift. The two differ in a number of important ways, however. In regeneration we come to God as a rebel; in entire sanctification we come as a child of God seeking a deeper commitment. In regeneration we repent of wrongdoing; in entire sanctification we consecrate our wills and lives for all God wants to do with us. In regeneration we come with the guilt of a sinful lifestyle; in entire sanctification we come with the frustration and hindrance of a sin principle that causes us to prefer self.

Biblical terminology indicates that entire sanctification happens in a moment of time. Symbols include a baptism (Acts 1:5), a sealing (2 Cor. 1:22), a crucifixion (Rom. 6:6), and a circumcision (Col. 2:11). None of these symbols suggest a long process. Verb usage in the original language also indicates an immediate experience. For example, the Greek aorist tense suggests an event occurring at a moment in time. Nevertheless, the immediate experience must give way to a lifetime of growth in grace. The difference between our spiritual progress before and after entire sanctification centers on the removal of the hindrance of self-sovereignty. We now have a new openness to God's direction in our lives.

Just prior to Jesus' ascension back to heaven from the Mount of Olives, He told His disciples, "You will receive power when the Holy Spirit comes on you; and you will be my witnesses in Jerusalem, and in all Judea and Samaria, and to the ends of the earth" (Acts 1:8). The apostle Peter summarized the lasting results of entire sanctification when he spoke to the Jerusalem Council, comparing the events at Cornelius's house with Pentecost. He said, "God, who knows the heart, showed that he accepted them by giving the Holy Spirit to them, just as he did to us. He made no distinction between us and them, for he purified their hearts by faith" (15:8-9). Together these two passages remind us that the lasting results of entire sanctification are power and purity.

Some refer to entire sanctification as "Christian perfection." Many people don't like that term because they misunderstand it to mean the entirely sanctified believe they are perfect. John Wesley also did not like the term for that reason. He continued to use it, however, because it's biblical. Jesus said, "Be perfect, therefore, as your heavenly Father is perfect" (Matt. 5:48). Since we are still human and continue to make mistakes and fall short of a perfect standard of conduct, what kind of "perfect" are we talking about? We mean perfect in motive and desire to please God.

Our actions are not flawless, but our intentions
are pure. We want to please God more than anything else in the world. Thus, as Mother Teresa
saw it, it is "doing the will of God with a smile."
Years of maturity and growth will bring our performance more into line with the desires of our
heart. God's Spirit continues to work with us to
complete that process.

using the truth to enrich your life

Sometime ago Sue and I visited our friends
Chip and Dana in southern California. Dana
showed us to the guest bedroom and said, "Make
yourselves at home." Now, she didn't really mean
it. She meant we had their permission to hang
our clothes in the closet and spread our personal
items around the bedroom. She also meant we
could use the iron or eat food from the kitchen.
But that's about it. When I'm at our home, I can
move the furniture, hang up new pictures, and
even knock out a wall if I want to enlarge a room.
I doubt if our friends would have appreciated our
rearranging their living room furniture or con-
ducting a garage sale of their possessions.

Something like our California visit exists in
our relationship with God. We invite Him into our
lives when we become a Christian. He is a guest
in our hearts. He has control of us—within the
limits we set. Our lives reflect His presence in
ways people can see. In time, however, we begin
to sense some resistance on our part to His addi-

tional requests for more control. We liked it just fine when His presence brought us peace and joy. Now He seems to be going a little too far by asking more than we care to give, like an Internal Revenue Service agent going through our financial records and wanting more tax money.

God's full control is the most liberating way to live.

God wants full control of our entire being. It comes down to a question of who is going to call the shots in life—us or God. If we retain control, we hinder further spiritual growth; the relationship suffers. If we give Him control, we fear He might ask us to do something we don't want to do, like becoming a missionary to Bugville or shaving our head. Then we wouldn't be happy. Nonsense. That is Satan's lie. God's full control is the most liberating way to live. It is a blessed abandonment of self-interest. God always has our best interest in mind, and He seeks to do more in us than we ever dreamed possible. That's what makes entire sanctification the greatest adventure in our spiritual journey. Giving God everything pays dividends for all eternity.

Frank Moore is vice president for academic affairs and dean of MidAmerica Nazarene University, where he has served since 1985. This chapter was first published in *More Coffee Shop Theology* (Kansas City: Beacon Hill Press of Kansas City, 1998), 67-70.

HOLINESS: CHRIST REIGNING WITHIN

william m. greathouse

I have been crucified with Christ; and it is no longer I who live, but it is Christ who lives in me. And the life I now live in the flesh I live by faith in the Son of God, who loved me and gave himself for me.   — Gal. 2:20

gal. 2:20 is paul's gospel of sanctification in all its dazzling beauty and divine complexity, set like a rare diamond between his gospel of justification (2:15-21) and the promised gift of the Spirit (3:1-14).

For Paul, as we have seen, justification and

sanctification are intimately related, just as Christ's death and resurrection are two phases of one event. To die with Christ to sin is to be simultaneously raised with Him to "new life [in] the Spirit" (Rom. 7:6; see 6:1-4).

Gal. 2:20 reminds us that God's purpose in our salvation is to one end: that in some divinely mysterious way Christ may be *reincarnate in our human flesh, living out His holy life in us!* (See Rom. 8:29.)

Such is the dynamism and the potency of the gospel of holiness: Christ reigning within, ruling all our powers and gradually transforming us into His own likeness, in the power of His life-giving Spirit (see 2 Cor. 3:18; 1 Cor. 15:45).

Let us now lift up the diamond of the gospel of holiness that we find in our text and view it from its three angles. Gal. 2:20 reveals that I have
a *sinful* self to be crucified with Christ,
a *human* self to be disciplined in Christ, and
a *true* self to be actualized in Christ.

a sinful self to be
crucified with Christ

The Greek reads literally, "With Christ I have been cocrucified; and lives no longer I *[egō]*, but lives in me Christ."

As members of Adam's fallen race we are born "curved in on ourselves," as Martin Luther said. We have a serious curvature of the heart. It is this sinful *egō* that God crucifies in the believer: the idolatrous self that dethrones God in its pride and rebellion (see Rom. 1:21-25).

All we mortals are, without exception, members of Adam's fallen race, who because of his defection have been cut off from the sanctifying grace of the Spirit. *Deprived* of the Spirit, we are morally *depraved.* Sin is a racial fact before it is an individual act. Fallen in Adam, we inevitably "individuate" as sinners.

Sin is a racial fact before it is an individual act.

In our own personal life *each* of us reenacts the Fall. The apostle speaks for us all when he writes, "Apart from the law sin lies dead. I was once alive apart from the law, but when the commandment came, sin revived and I died" (Rom. 7:8-10). At some point in our personal journey— we call it the age of moral accountability—each of us hears God's voice within, commanding, "Thou shalt not!" Without exception, because we are inwardly depraved, we inevitably disobey. It is thus that sin becomes *transgression.*

"Explain original sin in any way you choose," Professor Edward Ramsdell said in a university lecture; "you cannot explain it away; it is an empirical fact." Scripture says plainly, "All have sinned and fall short of the glory of God" (Rom. 3:23). That is the bad news.

Thank God, there is good news: "The saying is sure and worthy of full acceptance, that Christ Jesus came into the world to save sinners—of whom I am the foremost" (1 Tim. 1:15).

But since salvation is by grace apart from the works of the Law, and since the Law cannot produce a holy life but serves only to activate sin and turn it into transgression, and since where sin has abounded grace has all the more abounded (see Rom. 5:18-21), "What shall we say, then? Shall we go on sinning so that grace may increase?" In answer to this bogus logic the apostle resounds, "By no means! We died to sin; how can we live in it any longer?" (6:1-2, NIV). Rather than providing blanket forgiveness for all our sins "past, present, and future," justification *breaks the power of sin!*

The Old Testament guilt offering suggests a helpful illustration of justifying faith. An Israelite who had become conscious of guilt and was seeking forgiveness was to select as a guilt offering a ram without blemish from his flock and bring it to the priest. Associating himself with the victim, he must place his hand upon its head as a sign of a unity he wished to affirm and effect, while at the same time confessing the sins that had occasioned the sacrifice. As the blood flowed from the victim's throat, the sinner "died" in and with the sacrificial offering. The communion thus realized by sacrifice gave the believing Israelite access to the renewing and revitalizing forces released by contact with the altar, that is, with God, through his vicarious sacrifice.[1]

In like manner, when we come to Christ for pardon, we acknowledge that it was *our* sins that nailed _Him_ to the Cross. In repentance and faith, we _appropriate_ the death of Christ, His death _for_ our sin thereby becoming our death _to_ sin. This understanding of Christ's atoning sacrifice is the reason Paul utterly repudiates the notion that Christians can go on living in sin: "How can we who died to sin go on living in it?" (Rom. 6:2). That is to say, how can we _as Christians_ go on _living_ in sin, since we _as Christians_ have _died_ to sin?

Jesus is now Lord, but self would like to be prime minister!

A young woman who had quite a reputation for wild partying was powerfully converted in a gospel crusade. A few nights later one of her old friends called, saying, "We're having a bar-nothing party tonight. Will you go with me as my date?" to which she replied, "I'm sorry. I can't go —_I'm dead!_" There was then a click on the other end of the line. Such a death to sin, signed and sealed by baptism (see Rom. 6:3-4), is what it means to be scripturally converted. As Charles Wesley sings,

> He breaks the pow'r of canceled sin;
> He sets the pris'ner free.

Our sinful predicament, however, is deeper than the _compulsion to sinning_ that God heals in conversion. Even radical conversion does not resolve the sin problem (as we may think at first). Though sin no longer _reigns,_ every Christian soon discovers sin still _remains,_ as an _ego-bias_ rivaling Christ's reign within our hearts. Jesus is now Lord, but self would like to be prime minister!

This remaining "root" of sin is

the presupposition of all the exhortations and prayers for holiness in the Epistles (2 Cor. 7:1; 1 Thess. 4:4-8; 5:23-24),

the confession of all the great creeds of the Church, and

eventually the humble confession of every justified believer endeavoring to "have the mind of Christ" and "walk as Jesus did" (1 Cor. 2:16; 1 John 2:6, NIV).

Remaining sin has been defined variously, as

"a hard core of idolatrous self-love" (Richard S. Taylor),

"a residue of recalcitrancy" (E. Stanley Jones),

"the delusion of self-sovereignty" (Millard Reed),

"my claim to my right to myself" (Oswald Chambers).

"We have met the enemy, and he is us!" comics character Pogo says. The proper way to spell sin is to hyphenate it: *s-I-n*—at its heart is idolatrous self-love. As the old spiritual goes,

Not my brother, not my sister, but it's me, O Lord, Standin' in the need of prayer.

The remaining ego-bias that plagues the unsanctified believer demands a *deeper* death to sin —a death to *sin itself;* the death of "my claim to my right to myself." In a word, the holiness command is the imperative to *actualize my conversion.*

Paul exhorts the Roman Christians to "present" themselves to God, once and for all,[2] as those who have been brought from death to life. Returning to this gospel imperative a few verses later, he explains it in human terms because of their "natural limitations": "For just as you once presented your members as slaves to impurity and to greater and greater iniquity, *so now present your members as slaves to righteousness for sanctification*" (6:19, emphasis added). Oswald Chambers finds a mystery here—that some who were formerly such outbroken sinners choose now to be timid saints! The call is for a total abandonment of myself to God's sovereign claims upon my heart and life.

The sin that remains is clearly self-sovereignty: my determining how much of myself I will permit God to possess and purify. The call is for total self-abdication to God, *"for sanctification"*— what Wesley sometimes called "full sanctification." This sanctification is both the divine act of heart cleansing and the resulting life of holiness. The following passage makes this clear: "But now having been set free from sin, and having become slaves of God, you have your fruit to holiness, and the end, everlasting life" (Rom. 6:22, NKJV); or, "But now that you have been freed from sin and enslaved to God, the advantage you get is sanctification" (NRSV).

The complete self-giving that makes possible this full release of God's sanctifying power is beautifully foreshadowed in the self-dedication of the Hebrew slave who, not choosing to go out free in the year of jubilee, declares, "I love my master, my wife, and my children; I will not go out a free person" (Exod. 21:5). He then presents himself to his master, who pierces his ear with an awl, making him a "love slave" for life (see vv. 2-6). This is the servitude of perfect freedom.

It is in such an act of self-donation that Christ establishes His sanctifying reign in my heart, enabling me to say in all humility and praise to God: "I have been crucified with Christ; and it is no longer I who live, but it is Christ who lives in me" (Gal. 2:20).

a human self to be disciplined in Christ

Even though I have experienced a radical death to sin, and Christ now reigns in me in the power of the indwelling Spirit, my continued victory is guaranteed only as I maintain this vital relationship. "I have been crucified with Christ" is the perfect tense in Greek and has the force *"I have been and am now crucified with Christ."* The holy life is a moment-by-moment relationship maintained as I submit to the disciplines of the Spirit. "I say, walk by the Spirit," Paul writes later in Galatians, "and you will not carry out the desire of the flesh" (5:16, NASB).

The threat to continuing victory is posed by

my *natural* self that lives on beyond the crisis of full sanctification. The King James Version catches Paul's thought when it states, "I am crucified with Christ: *nevertheless I live*" (2:20, emphasis added). The repetition of "I" and "me" throughout the text underscores the survival of the essential self beyond the crucifixion of the sinful self. It is therefore a mistake to speak of the death of self; in crucifixion with Christ the self dies to sin. "I died, and I died ungraciously," one preacher declared, "but I died only to that which made me die."

Furthermore, the holy life is a life "in the flesh": When Paul says, "The life I now live *in the flesh* [but not *according* to the flesh] I live by faith in the Son of God, who loved me and gave himself for me" (v. 20, emphasis added), he means that I live the holy life in a flesh-and-blood body, with all its passions and desires—the same kind of body, incidentally, that the Son of God assumed in the Incarnation. It was as a true man that Jesus was "tempted in every way, just as we are—yet was without sin" (Heb. 4:15, NIV). As He lived a holy life in a physical body with all its urges, drives, and desires, so may we—by the power of the same Spirit who indwelt Him! The apostle asks, "Or do you not know that your body is a temple of the Holy Spirit within you, which you have from God, and that you are not your own? For you were bought with a price; therefore glorify God in your body" (1 Cor. 6:19-20).

Elsewhere Paul writes: "If you have been

raised with Christ, seek the things that are above. . . . For you have died, and your life is hidden with Christ in God. . . . Put to death, therefore, whatever in you is earthly: fornication, impurity, passion, evil desire, and greed" (Col. 3:1, 3, 5).

When Paul says in Romans, "You are not in the flesh" (8:9), he means Christians do not live "according to the flesh" (vv. 4-5, 12-13), do not have the "mind set on the flesh" (see vv. 5-7), in either self-indulgence or self-dependence (see vv. 1-7). Conversely, Paul writes, "The fruit of the Spirit is . . . self-control. . . . And those who belong to Christ Jesus have crucified the flesh with its passions and desires. If we live by the Spirit, let us also be guided by the Spirit" (Gal. 5:22-25).

"How can I live a holy life in a world like this?" a man asked the late Jack Ford, then rector of British Isles Nazarene College in Manchester, England.

"Do you believe Jesus Christ lived a holy life?" Ford countered.

"Of course," the man replied.

"The question, then, is this," Ford continued. "Will you permit Jesus Christ to live *His* holy life in you?"

That is the question.

The Scriptures clearly contain a doctrine of both *counteraction* and *suppression,* not of sin (which is destroyed by sanctifying grace) but of our bodily impulses that may lead to sin. In Rom. 8 Paul admonishes, "For if you are living according to the flesh, you must die; but if by the Spirit you are putting to death the deeds of the body, you will live" (v. 13, NASB). That is scriptural counteraction. Again Paul writes, "I buffet my body and make it my slave, lest possibly, after I have preached to others, I myself should be disqualified" (1 Cor. 9:27, NASB). That is scriptural suppression.

By *"sōma* (body)," a New Testament scholar writes, Paul means "the nearest equivalent of our word 'personality.'"[3] "The deeds of the body" we are commanded to "put . . . to death" are therefore our psychological as well as our physical impulses—all the mechanistic tendencies of the psyche (rationalization, projection, denial, and so on) along with the instinctual urges and drives of the body. The Spirit-filled believer remains a human ego with natural tendencies and still possesses what Freud called the "id," with its pressures and proddings. Since these impulses reside beneath the level of consciousness, they are morally neutral, but they may easily lead to sin and must therefore be controlled and subjugated by the power of the indwelling Spirit. If we "repress" them by denial, not only do we deceive ourselves, but also we become sick. By the Spirit we must "suppress" them by acknowledging them to God and permitting Him to give us victory over them (see 1 John 1:7-8).

W. E. Sangster has a helpful passage in his book *The Pure in Heart,* in which he insists that "life, as it bubbles out of the subconscious, is amoral, and should be regarded merely as instinct or 'reaction' until the conscious self identifies itself with the end desired." He continues:

When I feel a sudden stab of jealousy, is it I?—in the very instant that I feel it? Is it I, when some surge of pride stiffens my spirit? Is it I, in the moment when some carnal appetite stirs in my flesh?

Certainly, in that split second, it feels like me. . . . Is that carnality, pride, jealousy, self-pity or any other member of the dirty litter—is it mine?—mine the second that I feel it; mine whether I disown it or not?

I cannot feel that it is. As a conscious moral being, it is not mine till my will makes it mine. I have an amoral nature, with race and family memories and tendencies. But, as a person, and with the help of the Holy Ghost, the animal nature can be curbed, chained, subdued, mastered. No more of it need be admitted to my moral life than fellowship with God allows. In the moment it stirs in me, trying to wrest my moral life to what I judge to be evil, it is still only temptation. If I finger it awhile and glut my imagination in it, it becomes mine, even though it has not issued in a deed, because I have taken it as my own.

I will not take it as my own. I will learn from the saints how to assess it swiftly in the light of God and, seeing it to be evil, blast it with a prayer.

It was never my own. It was amoral instinct. It was only impulse bidding for moral stature. It was recognized in the white light of God in its evil tendency, and never passed the moral guard.[4]

The apostle John writes, "You are from God, little children, and have overcome them; *because greater is He who is in you than he who is in the world*" (1 John 4:4, NASB, emphasis added). Then later he adds, "And this is the victory that has overcome the world—our faith" (5:4, NASB).

a true self to be actualized in Christ: "yet not i, but Christ"

I once understood Paul to be saying in Galatians what Jesus said in the Gospels—that if I deny myself and take up my cross daily and follow Him, I will find *self-fulfillment* (see Luke 9:23-24).

Of course nothing is truer: the way of the Cross is indeed the way of personal fulfillment. Yet in fullest Christian perspective, self-fulfillment is only the *by-product* of crucifixion with Christ. The end God has in mind in our crucifixion with Christ is *the actualization of the divine self*—"not I, but Christ" (KJV). *Self-actualization* is the ideal of the so-called New Age movement; *Christ-actualization* is the goal of the gospel.

God's purpose in crucifying my pre-

Self-actualization is the goal of the New Age movement. Christ-actualization is the goal of the gospel.

tentious self is simply that *Christ may become re-incarnate in me* and live out *His* life of holy, loving servitude in *my* everyday, humdrum existence. Bill Bright shares with us his life in Christ:

> I usually awaken with a psalm of praise on my lips, with an attitude of thanksgiving: "Oh, Lord, I thank You that I belong to You. I thank You that You live within me, and I thank You that You have forgiven my sins. I thank You that I am a child of God. Now as I begin this day, as I continue throughout the day, I thank You that You walk around in my body, love with my heart, speak with my lips, and think with my mind. I thank You that, during the course of the day, You promised to do greater things through me than You did when You were here on earth. By faith I acknowledge Your greatness, Your power, Your authority in my life, and I invite you to do anything You wish in and through me."
>
> Then I slip out of bed on my knees, as a formal act of acknowledging His lordship.[5]

This identification with Christ is at once the secret and the simplicity of the holy life.

Have Thine own way, Lord! Have Thine own way!
Hold o'er my being absolute sway!
Fill with Thy Spirit till all shall see
Christ only, always living in me!
                                              —Adelaide A. Pollard

notes

1. Franz J. Leenhardt, *The Epistle to the Romans* (Cleve-

land and New York: World Publishing Company, 1957), 103-4.

    2. This is the force of the Greek aorist tense here in Rom. 6.

    3. J. A. T. Robinson, _The Body_ (London: SCM Press, 1952), 28.

    4. William E. Sangster, _The Pure in Heart_ (New York and Nashville: Abingdon Press, 1964), 235-36. This is the thesis of the late Nazarene general superintendent R. T. Williams in his book _Temptation: A Neglected Theme_ (Kansas City: Nazarene Publishing House, 1920).

    5. Bill Bright, _How to Walk in the Spirit_ (San Bernardino, Calif.: Campus Crusade for Christ, 1971), 47-48.

William M. Greathouse is a general superintendent emeritus in the Church of the Nazarene. This chapter was first published in _Love Made Perfect: Foundations for the Holy Life_ (Kansas City: Beacon Hill Press of Kansas City, 1997), 63-73.

A HOLY CHURCH

jeren rowell

much of my childhood was spent on the front pew of the Church of the Nazarene in a little lumber town in western Oregon. From my first-row vantage point, I witnessed my parents leading worship in various ways. One vivid memory is of a duet they sang, a gospel song popular in the United States in the mid-20th century called "On the Jericho Road." I loved hearing my parents sing together, but it never occurred to me that the whole idea of "room for just two" was inconsistent with New Testament discipleship.

I have learned a couple of things since then. One is that the Christian life is at its heart a community life. The other is that many Nazarenes still think of discipleship as a mostly personal or even a private matter. This individualism influences the way we think about and express the doctrine of holiness. We speak of holiness mostly in terms of personal piety. Little is said about the holiness of the church. Certainly the grace of entire sanctification is thoroughly personal, but it is not private. The New Testament vision of holiness finds its full meaning only as sanctified persons see themselves essentially as part of a sanctified church. Jesus' prayer for us is a corporate prayer: "Sanctify them by the truth. . . . May they . . . be one as we are one" (John 17:17, 21-22). Jesus expects that the perfect community of the Godhead will be reflected in the community of saints. The letters of Paul to the churches are replete with exhortations toward holiness that are corporate in nature (Rom. 13:8-10; 15:5-7; 1 Cor. 1:2; 12:12-13; Gal. 5:16-26; Eph. 1:1-14; 2:19-22; 4:1—5:20; Col. 3:12-17). The Scriptures seem to have in mind more than a simple collection of holy *ones*.

Jesus expects that the perfect community of the Godhead will be reflected in the community of saints.

There is a call to the community of faith for its life together to be characterized by holiness.

So an important question is, "How is biblical holiness corporate and not individual only?" There are many ways to answer that question. I suggest four ways that local congregations can grow in the understanding, experience, and practice of corporate holiness.

First, worship by local congregations must be firmly rooted in the historic Christian faith. Too often the worship of the community of faith is ordered around pragmatic concerns, or to put it plainly, around what will draw a crowd. Marva Dawn says, "So many decisions are being based on criteria other than the most essential—namely, that God be the Subject and Object . . . of our worship" *(A Royal "Waste" of Time)*. Holiness is nothing if not the change of life's focus from self to God. The acts of the worshiping community are essential to this understanding and experience.

The second needed focus is on Christian forgiveness. Of course the larger issue is love, which is central to the whole idea of holiness, but I emphasize forgiveness because what most damages authentic corporate holiness is unforgiveness. Christian relationships afford us ample opportunity for real experiences of self-sacrificing love, the essence of holiness. If we really believe what we say we believe about holiness, our relationships in the church should not so regularly remain broken by unforgiveness.

The third critical component for corporate holiness is unity. Christian unity is the indisputable sign that the people of God have surrendered their own interests to the Kingdom interest of serving God and neighbor.

The fourth element is service. Corporate holiness is much more than a group of Christians being pious. It is the community of faith actively serving each other and engaging a broken world with acts of sacrificial love and service.

It is important that all of us think about how
our personal lives reflect the holy life of Christ.
It's also important to think about how our congregations reflect the holiness of God. Discipleship
is not about "room for just two." True discipleship
and true holiness mean surrendering self-interest to the interests of the Kingdom. The sanctifying power of the Holy Spirit is at work in each
one who confesses Jesus as Lord. That power is
also at work in congregations of Christians who
make that confession together.

So not only do we sing, "In my life, Lord, be
glorified," but also we sing, "In our church, Lord,
be glorified."*

---

*"Lord, Be Glorified," by Bob Kilpatrick. Copyright 1978 Bob
Kilpatrick Music. Assigned 1998 to The Lorenz Corporation. All
rights reserved. International copyright secured.

Jeren Rowell is pastor of the Shawnee Church of the Nazarene
in Shawnee, Kansas. This article was first published in *Holiness
Today*, April 2002.

HOLINESS IN COMMUNITY

wesley d. tracy

whatever else the Christian Church may be, it is, first of all, a *worshiping community,* a family of faith.

The ideal for holy church relationships is the perfect community of the Persons of the Holy Trinity. Though we fall short of that holy ideal, we must keep it before us as we work, suffer, and pray together.

Nothing on earth, certainly no private spiritual discipline, can take the place of corporate worship. Nothing on earth is more important than the worship of God.

Worship is not primarily about us or our bundle of felt needs, wishes, or good intentions or our desire to escape the dull or threatening realities of life through a swooning spiritual experience. Worship is about God. We worship God because of who He is. The word *worship* comes from the

Anglo-Saxon *weorthscipe*—"worth-ship." God's worth, His worthiness, calls us to worship.

We are angels with only one wing. We can fly only by embracing each other.

Worship is not about performance. The worship leaders are not there to keep us amused and entertained; they are not performers fishing for double encores. They are to guide us in offering a holy sacrifice of worship to God.

John Wesley wrote, "All the children of God may united in love, notwithstanding their differences in opinion or modes of worship" (*Letters,* 5:116). A brick alone in a field is a hazard to bare toes and lawn mowers. But a brick joined with other bricks in a church building can hold up the cross, the pulpit, and the altar. Solitary Christians are like solitary bricks. Maria Harris had a point in *Fashion Me a People:* "A solitary Christian is no Christian; we go to God together or we do not go at all."

We are angels with only one wing. We can fly only by embracing each other.

This article was first published in *Holiness Today,* April 2002.

HOLINESS—
CORE
QUESTIONS,
STRAIGHT
ANSWERS

rob l. staples

Q. What is sanctification?

A. To sanctify means to make holy. Thus sanctification and holiness are synonymous terms. In its broadest sense, sanctification is the lifelong process of becoming the "saints" we are "called to be" (Rom. 1:7), "perfecting holiness out of reverence for God" (2 Cor. 7:1), and moving, by grace, toward

our destiny. That destiny is defined by the image
of God in which we were created (Gen. 1:27). In
sin we rejected our destiny. The *image* that is our
destiny is now defined by Jesus Christ, who is
"the image of the invisible God" (Col. 1:15) and
"the exact representation of his being" (Heb. 1:3).
Our destiny, then, is "to be conformed to the likeness of his Son" (Rom. 8:29) and into that image
we "are being transformed" (2 Cor. 3:18) as we
keep our destiny in view. That is what sanctification is all about.

Q. How and when does sanctification occur?

A. It is both gradual and instantaneous, a process
comprising definite stages. John Wesley said, "It
begins the moment we are justified. . . . It gradually increases from that moment . . . till, in another instant, the heart is cleansed from all sin, and
filled with pure love to God and man. But even
that love increases more and more . . . till we at-
tain 'the measure of the stature of the fullness of
Christ'" (*Works,* 6:509).

In the Wesleyan tradition, that which begins
"the moment we are justified" is called *initial
sanctification.* That which "gradually increases" is
progressive sanctification. Wesley's "another instant" in which the heart is cleansed and filled
with pure love is known as *entire sanctification.*
As that love "increases more and more," the *progressive* work of sanctification continues. There is

also a *final sanctification* at the resurrection when the scars left by sin are forever healed. So the word *sanctification* has different nuances of meaning regarding the time and manner in which it occurs.

Q. What difference will entire sanctification make in my life?

A. It is simply the difference between having started on the journey and proceeding no further versus being all that God wants you to be and receiving all that His grace has provided. Someone has said, "Even if you are on the right track, if you just sit there you will get run over!" So move on under the power of the Spirit!

Q. How is it different from just being a Christian?

A. "Just being a Christian?" What kind of question is that? Entire sanctification is not some à la mode topping on the pie! It is the pie itself. We do not become Christian and later get something extra that makes us even more and better than Christian. The New Testament norm for the Christian is the sanctified, cleansed, Spirit-filled, love-purified life. Of course there are stages in becoming a New Testament Christian, as noted above, and it is possible to live below the norm. A person who willfully settles for less than the norm can hardly be called a New Testament Christian.

Q. What is the difference between sanctification and consecration?

A. Consecration is the human part. It is our commitment toward our destiny of Christlikeness. Sanctification is God's part. Only God can make us holy in response to our consecration. In Romans 6:12-19, we are told to present ourselves to God (consecration), which leads to, or results in, holiness or sanctification, which is God's act.

Q. How will I know when I've been entirely sanctified?

A. You will know it when you have made a complete consecration, when you have held nothing back from God and are trusting Him to sanctify you. We are sanctified by faith and not by works. If you seek it by works, you are thinking you must *be* or *do* something first. Wesley said, "Expect it *by faith*, expect it *as you are*, and expect it *now!*" (*Works*, 6:53).

Q. What happens when I blow it?

A. That depends on you. We who drive cars usually carry a spare tire. We hope we never have to use it. But if we have a "blowout," we have two choices: We can sit in the car bemoaning our failure and quit the journey, or we can get out, change the tire, and, without too much lost time, proceed toward our destination. In 1 John 2:1-2, we are given, as it were, a "spare tire" in Jesus Christ who "speaks to the Father in our defense." That is what Wesley called "the repentance of believers," which is required in every stage of the Christian's life (*Works*, 5:157). Of course we must not presume by taking sin lightly.

Q. How can I be expected to be perfect even as God is perfect (Matt. 5:48)? Does this mean I cannot sin?

A. Light is shed on this command by its context (vv. 43-48). Being perfect as God is perfect means loving our enemies, praying for those who persecute us, and practicing justice toward both the evil and the good, toward both the righteous and the unrighteous.

The New Testament Greek word translated *perfect* may also be translated *mature*. It is a dynamic, not static, term. It does not denote the perfection of a flawless diamond with its facets sparkling in the light but rather the perfection of a growing, active, learning human being. The perfect are not the flawless but the maturing. To be perfect is to be fully turned toward God in the spirit of the psalmist (Ps. 139:23-24) and fully turned toward the neighbor in love and compassion.

Being perfected in love does not mean we can never sin. But by God's grace it is possible not to sin.

Rob L. Staples is professor of theology emeritus at Nazarene Theological Seminary in Kansas City. Words in this Q and A forum such as *sin, holiness, sanctification,* and *perfection* are explained in his book, *Words of Faith: An Easy Reference to Theological Terms* (Kansas City: Beacon Hill Press of Kansas City, 2001). This article was first published as "Editor's Forum" in *Holiness Today,* April 2002.

BECOMING MORE CHRISTLIKE

frank moore

Growth is the only evidence of life.

—John Henry Newman

> *"Like newborn babies, crave pure spiritual milk, so that by it you may grow up in your salvation"* (1 Pet. 2:2).
>
> *"Grow in the grace and knowledge of our Lord and Savior Jesus Christ. To him be glory both now and forever! Amen"* (2 Pet. 3:18).

Jesus compared the christian life to physical life. The birth, growth, and development of a baby into a mature adult parallels the spiritual pilgrimage of a person who becomes a Christian. Most of the Bible's message aims to help us develop our greatest potential toward Christlikeness while we live on earth.

thinking about the truth in everyday language

Our life on earth starts with small beginnings. I still find it hard to believe that my 6-foot, 3-inch son once lay in my palms. Life requires constant care at the beginning. Sue and I got very little sleep those first few months as we cared for our baby around the clock. Life requires frequent and balanced nourishment. Kids can eat like bottomless pits; I still wonder where Brent puts it all! Growth comes in small, unnoticed changes. Brent's grandparents, who visit a few times each year, notice his growth better than we do. Growth results in a full-size adult body with maturity.

Jesus said the Christian life begins in new birth, grows, and develops in much the same ways as our children grow and develop physically. Phineas F. Bresee observed, "God's child, like all children, begins a babe. He has to be nursed, fed with milk, cared for, taught, trained, corrected, brought on to manhood."[1] The goal is spiritual maturity. However, growth continues until we go to heaven, where it will continue on a higher level forever. The Bible speaks often about our need to grow and develop in the faith. This prompted Paul to pray in Eph. 3:17-18 that believers, "being rooted and established in love, may have power, together with all the saints, to grasp how wide

and long and high and deep is the love of Christ."
He further urged that they would not be spiritual
infants, swayed by every doctrine that came
along. Rather, they were to "grow up into him who
is the Head, that is, Christ" (4:15). In Gal. 5:22-23,
Paul lists the fruit that a mature Christian should
display: "love, joy, peace, patience, kindness, goodness, faithfulness, gentleness and self-control."

"To acquire self-discipline and self-control, you
start with a single step: you decide that you can
do it."
                                    —Norman Vincent Peale

   Peter addressed a similar concern when he
said, "Make every effort to add to your faith goodness; and to goodness, knowledge; and to knowledge, self-control; and to self-control, perseverance; and to perseverance, godliness; and to
godliness, brotherly kindness; and to brotherly
kindness, love. For if you possess these qualities
in increasing measure, they will keep you from
being ineffective and unproductive in your
knowledge of our Lord Jesus Christ" (2 Pet. 1:5-8).
   So what are the elements necessary to the
spiritual growth that the Bible outlines? The following is a partial list:
   1. *Participate in all the means of grace, such as*
      prayer, Bible reading, meditation, corporate
      worship, the Lord's Supper, Christian fellow-
      ship, and fasting. To this list should be
      added listening to Christian music and

reading Christian literature. Make your
faith the organizing principle of your life.

2. *Practice the presence of God in your life every day.* Talk with Him throughout the day
as you would talk with your closest friend.
Listen for His voice directing you, and obey
Him. Stop doing what He tells you to stop
doing, and start what He tells you to start.
Welcome new light from God.

3. *Discipline your life to make it consistent with
your commitment to Christ.* This discipline
applies to areas like eating habits, entertainment choices, usage of time, choice of
friends, responsibility to commitments,
keeping of your word, honesty in business
dealings, responsibility with your money,
and attitudes. Remember the words of Norman Vincent Peale: "To acquire self-discipline and self-control, you start with a single step: you decide that you can do it."[2] You
won't always find yourself on top of every
situation. Sometimes you will stumble along
the way. When you do, talk to the Lord about
it, get back up, and keep walking with
Christ. Ask Him to help you help yourself.

4. *Learn to cope with life's daily circumstances.*
Some days you get the elevator, other days
the shaft. Learn not to gauge your level of
spiritual maturity on how well things happen to be going at the time. You can be
close to God when circumstances are col-

lapsing around you and drifting when everything is going well. Coping skills are as important to successful Christian living as spiritual experiences. Anticipate problems before they become unsolvable. Remember the Russian proverb: "Little drops of water wear down a big stone."[3]

5. *Commit to the Lord your past failures, your appetites, weaknesses, temptations, the failures of others, and situations you cannot change.* Leave all these things in God's hands, and talk to Him about them as often as they come to your mind. Becoming a Christian does not solve all of your problems any more than winning a sweepstakes brings you ultimate happiness. It does give you spiritual resources for dealing effectively with them. Get help from trusted Christian friends or counselors if you need it. God may work through them to help you.

Open all of your life to Kingdom priorities.

6. *Open all of your life to Kingdom priorities.* This includes giving time and money to the cause of Christ. Give your life away in service to others. It won't seem like an obligation, but rather a welcomed opportunity, as Jesus described in Matt. 25:31-46. His followers fed the hungry, took in strangers, clothed the needy, and cared for the sick and imprisoned without even noticing what

they did. It was just a natural outgrowth of
their faith. Martin Luther King Jr. reminded, "Everybody can be great . . . because
anybody can serve. You only need a heart
full of grace. A soul generated by love."[4]
Central to all growth is Christlikeness. Paul
says believers have "the mind of Christ" (1 Cor.
2:16). The more time we spend with Him reading
His Word and Christian literature, listening to
music about Him, and having fellowship with
other believers, the more like Him we become. We
are adopted into His family, and we take on the
family resemblance. It becomes natural for us to
prefer the things He prefers and shy away from
what displeases Him. Our actions, attitudes, intentions, and motives fall in line with His purposes. As Paul again said, "I want to know Christ and
the power of his resurrection and the fellowship
of sharing in his sufferings, becoming like him in
his death" (Phil. 3:10).

using the truth to enrich your life

Christian songs and sermons sometimes put
us under bondage about this growth process.
You've probably heard the same things I have: "If
you don't love Jesus more today than you did yesterday, then you don't love Jesus"; "Life with Jesus
gets sweeter every day"; "Christians who live close
to God will grow by leaps and bounds." Rather un-
realistic, I would say. I can't honestly claim that I
feel closer to God today than I did yesterday or

that my daily spiritual growth blows the top off the charts. Orel Hershiser said it well: "Christianity is called a spiritual walk. It's not a run and it's not a jog. It's a walk you do from day to day."[5]

I can see growth across the years the same way I watched our child grow. Looking at his annual school pictures proves the point. Snail-paced changes add up. Look back over your spiritual journey since you accepted Christ as your Savior. Have you grown in any of the areas discussed in this chapter? Probably. The "then" and "now" pictures might even be as different as dark and noonday. Don't let the devil defeat you over growth areas that God points out in your life. Let those points of growth serve as proof that you are spiritually alive. God is with you, and He will continue to develop you until the day He calls you home. Remember Phineas F. Bresee's encouragement: "There is no end to the possibilities of a soul in grace. The love of God is measureless, and we may even know more and more of His boundless grace."[6]

God will continue to develop you until the day He calls you home.

notes

1. *The Quotable Bresee,* ed. Harold Ivan Smith (Kansas City: Beacon Hill Press of Kansas City, 1983), 34.

2. Stevens W. Anderson, ed., *Compact Classics,* vol. 3 (Salt Lake City: Lan C. England, 1994), 443.

3. Ibid., 434.

4. Ibid., 441.

    5. Billy Hughey and Joyce Hughey, *A Rainbow of Hope* (El Reno, Okla.: Rainbow Studies, 1994), 40.

    6. Smith, *Quotable Bresee,* 35.

This chapter was first published in *More Coffee Shop Theology* (Kansas City: Beacon Hill Press of Kansas City, 1998), 72-75.

HOLINESS

passing the baton
to a new generation

WHO CARES ABOUT HOLINESS ANYHOW?

gordon j. thomas

the preacher lifted his hand and hushed
the congregational singing. The organist carried
on, playing quietly in the background. Once again
we were invited to put our "all on the altar" and to
settle the matter with God by getting up out of our
seats and kneeling at the front of the church.
Since the meeting seemed to have gone on for
hours already and there seemed little likelihood
that we'd be allowed home anytime soon unless
someone responded, the pressure was on. There
was also some inner pressure in my mind. The
preacher had vividly contrasted the peace and joy

of the sanctified life with the peaks and troughs of the unsanctified Christian life, where God and sin competed for Lordship.

At the time, I was in the throes of adolescence, with all the raging hormones and violent mood swings that characterize it. A constant mountain-top Christian experience sounded very appealing, but many trips to the altar had proved it to be elusive. If I went forward one more time, made my total consecration to God even more total, and exercised even more faith that God keeps His promises, maybe this time the effect would last for more than two or three days.

what about my parents' generation?

It all seemed so much simpler for my parents' generation. My dad had come to Christ just after World War II and had been a Nazarene pastor for more than 30 years. Throughout my teen years, we argued constantly about everything from soccer to sanctification. My high school pretensions to intellectual sophistication clashed daily with the simple certainties of his profound faith.

As is true for many first-generation Christians, the transformation in my father's life when he accepted the gospel was enormous. From my perspective, most of the prominent older Christians I knew shared both a conviction that the holiness message was right and a passion to convey its importance. Their sense of urgency must have branded me for life. Even when I could make neither head nor tail of the apparent gap between theory and practice, I knew I could never rest until I thought things through and closed the gap.

God, in His mercy, met me on several occasions in life-changing ways.

Like many of my generation, I eventually became disillusioned with my church's rendition of the message of holiness because it failed to deliver the goods. There seemed to be a constant discrepancy between the ideal Christian life of total commitment, heart purity, and spiritual victory of the old-timers and my life in the real world.

If that were the end of my story, it would hardly be worth mentioning. But God, in His mercy, met me on several subsequent occasions in life-changing ways. In addition, and very significantly, the opportunity for formal study of the Bible and doctrine eventually came my way. It gave me tools with which to critique my spiritual heritage and to reformulate it for myself in words and concepts I could understand and follow.

what about my generation?

Despite my wife's unflagging efforts to forestall the ravages of time on me, I am now middle-aged. As I consider the young people with whom I grew up in the Church of the Nazarene, it seems that our generation in Britain is clearer about what it *doesn't* believe about holiness than what it *does* believe. We grew up hearing and singing the vocabulary of entire sanctification as "a second definite work of grace," but off the top of my head I can't think of a single one of my peers who gives clear-cut testimony to "getting into the blessing" as our forebears did.

what about the next generation?

And what of the younger generation? My children are ages 20 and 16, and I would be astonished if either of them could give the standard account of "second-blessing holiness" that was drummed into my generation. I sometimes lead seminars at district youth camps and retreats, and I see their generation torn between the pleasure-seeking of contemporary youth culture and an idealism that wants to change the world by tackling poverty and saving the environment. Where does holiness feature in their worldview? Not very prominently, I suspect. In most cases they seem not to have been given even a stereotype of holiness preaching that might spark the expected teenage rebellion.

Who cares about holiness anyhow? If I may oversimplify, I say this: my parents' generation was clear on holiness doctrine and cared passionately about it; my generation found the disparity between the holiness rhetoric and the reality too much to swallow; and my children's generation neither knows the doctrine nor cares about the experience. Could it be that we are only one generation away from losing entirely the distinctive emphasis on Christian holiness that presumably is our very reason for existing as a separate denomination? And even if we do care about holiness, does it make any kind of sense to us?

As I understand it, the mission of the Church of the Nazarene is to spread the message of Christian holiness not simply through its own ranks but also throughout the wider Body of Christ. However, if we cannot convince even ourselves of the validity of the holiness message, what chance is there of persuading the rest of the Christian Church that holiness is for all and for now?

is there a way forward?

David was awkward and uncomfortable when he faced Goliath in Saul's armor. He knew intuitively that he would be better off fighting with his own tried-and-tested weapons. I suspect that hand-me-down doctrines, sermons, and testimonies from our spiritual ancestors leave many younger Nazarene preachers and teachers feeling as vulnerable and ineffectual as David. What do we need, then, to be equipped to promote the message of holiness with conviction?

First, we need a fresh sense of *the nature of holiness.* It is not first and foremost a spiritual or emotional experience of a particular type. Nor is it primarily an ethical lifestyle characterized by specific forms of "unworldly" behavior—staying away from bars, refusing to wear jewelry or

We need to be gripped in both head and heart with the necessity of holiness.

makeup, avoiding mixed bathing, and the like. The absolute heart of the matter is that God alone is holy in himself, and all human holiness derives entirely from an unclouded relationship with Him.

Second, we need to be gripped in both head and heart with *the necessity of holiness.* In Leviticus 19, God commanded the people of Israel to be holy because He is holy. Many Christian traditions have interpreted this as a challenge to the spiritual elite to aim higher than the rest of us. However, the command is addressed to *"all* the congregation of the people of Israel" (v. 2, RSV, emphasis added). Holiness is not for the few but for all.

All Christian traditions agree that all believers will be holy in heaven, but many cast serious doubt on the extent to which people can be holy here and now. In Moses' day, the Israelites had no formal doctrine of an afterlife and of heaven and hell. They therefore could have understood the command to be holy as applying only to the here and now. Holiness is for all, it is for now, and it is a divine command, not a request or suggestion.

Third, we have to come to grips with *the nitty-gritty of holiness.* The theologians and biblical scholars can quibble about the doctrinal niceties, but we ordinary Christians want to know what we need to do or not do to live a holy life. My primary concern is to lead people into the fullness of Christian experience, and I find it helpful to run through a mental checklist to see whether the following components are all in place:

1. Radical repentance
2. Complete cleansing
3. Total consecration
4. Utter receptivity to the Holy Spirit
5. Ready acceptance of discipline
6. Constant vigilance
7. Right relationships

John Oswalt opens his recent book *Called to Be Holy* with a powerful warning: "The fate of the Christian Church in America and around the world depends upon what the Church does with the biblical doctrine of holiness." Insofar as we Nazarenes are part of the worldwide Christian Church, so does our fate. Insofar as we are guardians of this precious doctrine, we hold in our hands the fate of other Christians too. It's about time we got serious again about holiness!

Gordon J. Thomas lives in Manchester, England, where he is a lecturer in biblical studies at Nazarene Theological College—Manchester. This article was first published in *Holiness Today*, January 2002.

Holiness Defined for a New Generation

frank moore

when I run the videotape of my life back several years, I recall an interesting conversation I had with the woman who ordered textbooks for the university where I'd just started my career as a professor. The newness of it all excited me: a new job, a new location, and a new day for the theology department as I moved in fresh from graduate school. I walked over to the university bookstore one morning to order a new textbook for my theology class. The former professor of the class had told me it was time for a face-lift, with a new teacher and a new text.

I'll never forget the troubled look on the woman's face when I told her I wanted to change our theology textbook. Our casual conversation continued for a few minutes, and then her question finally exploded. "God doesn't change. The Bible doesn't change. So why do you want to change our theology?"

I spent the next several minutes trying to explain that though our basic beliefs about God and our relationship with Him do not change, the way we state those beliefs does change with each new generation. Just as styles of houses, clothes, hair, and cars constantly change, so does the way we express our faith. I'm not sure the bookstore clerk believed me, but she ordered the new theology textbook anyway!

Ever since that trip to the bookstore, I've been continually reminded of the importance of updating our expressions of faith for each new generation. I'm also reminded that there's a right way and a wrong way to go about it. Theological liberals have taken the wrong approach. They frequently update their faith statements and toss the former ones out the door like a Christmas tree on January 2. They make little or no attempt to preserve a faith heritage. In time, their belief system is transformed into something entirely different from what it used to be. A better approach translates the timeless gospel message into the fresh language of the new day while remaining true to the biblical text and the heritage of our faith. This approach challenges contemporary minds with the claims of the gospel set in everyday, common language.

The time has arrived for us to translate the biblical message of holiness for a new generation. The mere word *holiness* scares some people. It really shouldn't. Holiness is not just an abstract concept, a theory to be proved, or a doctrine to be dissected. Neither is it an argument won by stringing together a whole ream of Bible verses. Holiness describes a way of living made possible through intimate personal relationship with God. It speaks of life and relationship, not letter and law, not doctrine and theory. That changes the way we look at it.

Holiness describes a way of living made possible through intimate personal relationship with God.

Over the years, an entire vocabulary has sprung up in the discussion of holiness. Many new words emerged in the process. Sometimes the meanings of the words have about a hair's width of distance between them, requiring a microscope and tweezers to separate them. Sometimes the distinctions matter; sometimes they don't. Either way, many of the words scare people. So we must find a way to talk about this relationship between God and His children without getting caught up in the tornado of abstract concepts and theological jargon. We must deliver this biblical message of holiness to our day with words people understand. At the same time, we must remain true to the Scriptures and the faith heritage passed to us.

So what are the basics of the holiness message?

1. God is a holy God, and He desires holy children. God says, "Be holy because I, the LORD your God, am holy" (Lev. 19:2). He wants a great life for us. He wants us to know only joy without sin's heartache. He wants us to do right.

2. God created humanity with a special quality. He flung a million stars in the sky across a million miles. He created planets beyond our wildest imagination. He created earth's plant life, animal life, and sea life both large and small. But when He created humanity, He included a unique quality—free will. We can choose to love and obey God, or we can choose to break His heart. It's our call.

3. We used our free will to disobey God. Adam and Eve started the downward spiritual slide of humanity in the garden Fall. Humanity has carried on the tradition ever since. The choice to reject God created a radical change in the hearts of the first parents and in the hearts of all of their future children. The spiritual infection of a sin nature spread quickly throughout the entire human race, manifesting itself most often in the form of self-preference. Instead of preferring God's will and plan, we now prefer our own. We want to do our thing our way.

4. The good news of the gospel message is twofold: *(a)* God can forgive us of our past sins when we repent and confess them; and *(b)* He can also change our hearts from within and re-orient our fallen nature so we can return to His will and plan for our lives. He does so by healing us of the "self-preference" infection with which we are born into the world. As we continue to fellowship with God, our hearts remain cleansed from self-preference. We can then be what God wants us to be, not by ourselves but by the strength and power of His Holy Spirit who lives within us. Those are the keys to full salvation from sin: forgiveness for acts of sinning and a change of heart that removes the inclination to sin in the first place.

5. Because of this twofold truth, sin does not leave us hopelessly programmed to repeat our past sinfulness over and over for as long as we live. We are not doomed always to prefer our own ways to God's ways. The holiness message reminds us that sin's addictive power is not greater than God's healing power. Many Christians believe that once we touch sin to our lips, we're thrown into a hopeless cycle of recurrent sinning that not even God can change. Not so! God's power can decisively break sin's hold over us and renew us from within so we can continue to live every day as His child. In this way, we please Him and live according to the plan He had for us when He placed us in the garden. This goes a

long way in undoing the damage our hearts incurred in the Fall.

6. We participate in God's salvation plan. In order for Him to heal us of the infection, we must surrender the control center of life to Him. We must let Him have complete control of everything we are or hope to be: our past, present, and future, our hopes, dreams, goals, and aspirations. He gets the keys to every door in our heart and life.

The concept of sanctification is rich with meaning throughout Scripture, occurring more than 1,100 times.

7. God asks us to offer ourselves back to Him. Paul wrote, "Therefore, I urge you, brothers, in view of God's mercy, to offer your bodies as living sacrifices, holy and pleasing to God—this is your spiritual act of worship" (Rom. 12:1). We call this offer consecration. We make ourselves available to God as part of our worship.

8. God accepts our offer by sanctifying us. Paul speaks of this in 1 Thessalonians 5:23-24: "May God himself, the God of peace, sanctify you through and through. May your whole spirit, soul and body be kept blameless at the coming of our Lord Jesus Christ. The one who calls you is faithful and he will do it." The concept of sanctification is rich with meaning throughout Scripture, occurring more than 1,100 times. It's all that God does in us to restore our hearts to the way He created us to be—

and, deep down, the way we really want to be as we relate to our Heavenly Father and others. God's work of sanctification in us leads to a new availability to all He wants for us.

My time's up, but there's much more to say about holiness:

- God's timing in sanctifying us
- What sanctification does for us
- What sanctification does not do for us
- What happens in a moment of time compared with what happens through a lifetime of growth in grace

But when it's all said and done, in ancient language or new, holiness is more about Christlikeness than anything else. As Hebrews 12:2 puts it, "Let us fix our eyes on Jesus, the author and perfecter of our faith, who for the joy set before him endured the cross, scorning its shame, and sat down at the right hand of the throne of God." So fix your eyes on Jesus, and live His plan for your life.

Author Frank Moore recently wrote *Breaking Free from Sin's Grip: Holiness Defined for a New Generation*. It contains material that expands on the ideas discussed in this article and is available from Beacon Hill Press of Kansas City. This article was published in *Holiness Today*, January 2002.

HOLINESS: EXPERIENCE OR RELATIONSHIP?

h. ray dunning

"i was entirely sanctified 100 times!"
declared one enthusiastic witness in her public
testimony. Obviously she exaggerated, but her
words set me to thinking about the understanding
of "entire sanctification" that would lead to such a
declaration. While I cannot so state dogmatically, I
suspect her confession sprang from identifying
entire sanctification with a particular kind of tem-
porary and momentary "experience" that has to be
repeated frequently to stay current.

J. O. McClurkan, founder of Trevecca Nazarene
University, did not fit the mold of the typical
preacher of the 19th-century Holiness Movement. In fact, he often was considered not quite

orthodox in terms of the standard teachings of that movement. This may have been partly due to his Cumberland Presbyterian background, but I believe it largely arose from his close acquaintance with and brutal honesty about the realities of personal religious experience.

McClurkan had discovered considerable instability and dryness among the Holiness people of his day and attributed this outcome to their having sought an "experience" or "the blessing" rather than the "Blesser." While such language was typical at that time, McClurkan seemed to have deeper insight into its implications than many of his contemporaries who perpetually spoke of the doctrine and "experience" of sanctification.

Entire sanctification involves establishing a special relationship that holds the possibility of growth and development.

Stated in more modern language, McClurkan pointed out that entire sanctification involves establishing a special relationship that holds the possibility of growth and development and is not invalidated by the absence of certain feelings or even by occasional failures along the way.

One of the more difficult issues of holiness theology in the 19th and 20th centuries was the relation between the moment of beginning and the lifelong process that is indigenous to human existence. Too often, proponents gravitated to one extreme or the other. Some ended up putting "all their eggs in one basket," resulting in a stultifying concept of the religious life. Others saw only a progressive growth toward the holiness ideal.

When we recognize, as J. O. McClurkan did, that the "moment of experience" is only the beginning point for a life of continuous development through increased knowledge and added grace (2 Pet. 3:18), the religious life takes on an increased aura of romance, challenge, and excitement.

In explaining the doctrine of Christian holiness, we usually refer to John Wesley, since his particular formulations of the deeper Christian life are the fountainhead of the modern holiness movement. When we examine his teachings carefully, rather than selectively, we find him in full sympathy with this balanced understanding of the Christian experience. As he put it, there is no "perfection of degrees," that is, perfection that does not know continual increase. And he rightly interpreted the content of the holy life to be increasing conformity to the image of God as embodied in Jesus Christ.

Recent biblical and theological scholars almost universally recognize this view of the "process" of sanctification. Furthermore, the "image of God" that is the ideal of the sanctified life is generally now seen as a set of relations that includes a relation to God, to other persons, and to one's possessions. All of life is given character by the way we relate to these realities. A wrong relation defines sin, which makes sin a perversion of God's intention for human persons. Therefore sanctification is rightly interpreted as a humanizing relationship, and, like all relationships, it may be "perfect" at any one stage of development but can deepen and enlarge indefinitely with increased knowledge and experience. John Wesley himself saw sanctification as beginning at the new birth and continuing not only through all of life but through all eternity as well.

In a philosophy text, a writer once commented that his father remained alive as long as he lived. That wisdom became a compulsion for me, challenging me both intellectually and spiritually. If taken seriously, such a way of life could eliminate the stale or backward-looking character that marks too many folks who "experienced the second blessing" in their early years. Instead, such folks would leave behind "the elementary principles" and "go on to perfection" (Heb. 6:1, NKJV).

H. Ray Dunning is professor emeritus of theology and philosophy at Trevecca Nazarene University. This article was first published in *Holiness Today*, December 2001.

To Serve the Present Age

jan simonson lanham

ever since the jews in palestine faced
the challenge of spreading the gospel into the
Gentile world, the Church has grappled with how
to translate the gospel to each new culture and to
each new generation. We in the Church of the
Nazarene understand the imperatives of this
transmission process and the tremendous challenges posed by a new millennium. We need to
employ as many means as possible to challenge
people with what it means to be Christian, to embrace holiness, and to be missional.

With this task of transmitting the core values
to the next generation in mind, the Church of the
Nazarene brought together a representative
group of Nazarenes to study, discuss, and offer
suggestions as we enter this new millennium. The
passing of core values to the next generation
hinges on a number of important dynamics. The

task force identified some of those dynamics and the actions they imply:

Cross-cultural. Just as the Jews needed to understand the Gentile culture and language, we, too, need to understand the cultures around us. We live in a global environment; all of the world's cultures are potentially at our own doorstep. The mission field is no longer "over there" but next door.

Generational differences add to the complexity of translating the faith to children and grandchildren. Have we taken the time to listen to our youth? What drives them? What concerns them? How do we speak their language in such a way that they will capture the vision of the need for a personal relationship with Christ?

The church has the crucial task of communicating the holiness message with clarity and care to those who represent global and generational diversities. We must be much more intentional about translating the holiness distinctive into language that this generation can understand and appropriate. It is extremely important that we use language that expresses the concepts of holiness in relational terms for this and future generations.

Postmodern. Using the North American cultural scene as an example, we understand that this current generation faces specific realities. Adolescents are coming of age in a pluralistic society that offers seemingly endless choices. They have grown up with the expectation that their lives will operate from freedom, choice, and autonomy. Their attention and commitment is pulled from many directions. Yet this generation also seeks a personal, spiritual connection. They are intensely relational and willing to invest their lives in substantive commitments.

Therefore the church needs to do everything it can to articulate its identity clearly and live out its incarnational witness in integrity and love. We must demonstrate that the church is worth embracing.

Caring relationships and personal commitments. We know that each new generation must choose to accept God's grace and forgiveness and enter into a personal saving and sanctifying relationship with the Lord. The Church of the Nazarene has the continuing opportunity to offer children and adolescents a sense of belonging through warm and caring relationships, a sense of the purpose and meaning of life as we communicate and live out the gospel, and occasions to grow spiritually and personally as maturing persons through whom God can work.

We therefore must encourage intergenerational experiences in the local church to help our

The church needs to do everything it can to articulate its identity clearly and live out its incarnational witness in integrity and love.

adolescents connect meaningfully with adults and witness the faith lived out before them. Connecting with adults outside their families through mentoring, missions, service, and other such opportunities can be crucial for spiritual and emotional development. Do children and adolescents truly feel they are a vital part of the church community? Are they seeing the adults around them growing in their own spiritual lives? Ministry to children and youth should not be the exclusive role of the children's pastor or youth pastor. The whole church needs to be engaged in these ministries.

We cannot assume that each new generation will choose faith out of obligation to the previous generation.

Holistic. Passing core values to the next generation takes place both formally through instruction and informally through environment. Transmitting the message from one generation to another is not solely the work of curricula, although clearly articulated beliefs and excellent curricular resources are vital. We cannot assume that each new generation will choose faith out of obligation to the previous generation. The choice comes best in an atmosphere that is relational, incarnational, intentional, and authentic. It is a two-way negotiation: one generation seeks to transmit passion for the faith to the next, and the younger generation translates and appropriates the faith anew. In this process the faith tradition is regenerated. Can we hear how the younger generation is appropriating the faith and learn from their experience as well?

We must encourage our youth to participate actively in the church that welcomes them, models authentic Christian relationships for them, and provides them with meaningful connections and opportunities to serve. We do this best when our churches are healthy and focused on living out the values of the Kingdom before each other and the world.

Enculturation. Passing core values to the next generation involves both acquiring a faith and acquiring a culture. Enculturation takes place continuously in every arena of our lives. Therefore, the Church of the Nazarene must proactively, intentionally become part of this enculturation process.

The local church must take up the challenge to recognize developmental transitions in the lives of families (birth, entering grade school, middle school, high school, etc.) within the church setting. Rites of passage and other traditions have tremendous power to shape us psychologically and spiritually. They give us an identity and bind us together as one. Rituals, traditions, and rites of passage are a God-given means by which the adult generation may pass on its core values to the next generation. When tradition is valued and taken seriously, it sets the boundaries for our lives, our values, and our faith. We believe that God desires to infuse these rituals and traditions with life-transforming power, making them opportunities for spiritual decision and growth. Children and adolescents should participate actively in worship and in rituals of the church year as a way to learn the great themes of the faith.

Family. Passing core values to the next generation takes place almost exclusively within the context of family—church family and/or domestic family. We need to reinvigorate the image of the family, both as it relates to our earthly families and to the sense of connectedness within the family of God. Family imagery cuts across cultural boundaries and speaks powerfully to each one of us.

In a society that endures so much disconnection, the church can encourage connections among parishioners of all ages by helping families become stronger and providing a nurturing environment that is like family. We also need to be sensitive to those whose families are not present and incorporate them into the life of the church.

We want to encourage families to see themselves anew as the primary spiritual nurturer to their members. Families need to feel that they have the knowledge, resources, and opportunities to incorporate their faith into their everyday practices. They need to see that their role is pivotal in encouraging, teaching, and living out the faith before the younger generation. Our families must know that they are not alone and that they can find encouragement, support, and challenge within their local faith community. The local church can minister to families through small groups, solid teaching, lay leadership training, meaningful worship, prayer support, and instructional opportunities, to name a few. We also must produce creative materials that can help parents address spiritual topics at home. While children's ministry and youth ministry are important adjuncts to this process, they must not, and indeed cannot, take the place of what is accomplished in the home. As a church we need to help families gain a vision for their role and feel equipped to follow through on their task.

Our families must know that they are not alone and that they can find encouragement, support, and challenge within their local faith community.

We cannot take this transmission process for granted. It will not happen by accident. Speaking with "the tongues of men and of angels" (1 Cor. 13:1) will not be enough either. Our faith will be passed from one generation to the next as the vitality of our faith and our experience of grace and mercy are lived out in authentic, life-affirming, loving relationships. Only then will others see Je-

sus working with us and through us and know
that they, too, may experience that wonderful
journey.

Jan Simonson Lanham is professor of psychology at Eastern
Nazarene College in Quincy, Massachusetts, a licensed therapist
in private practice, and a member of the General Board of the
Church of the Nazarene. This article first appeared in *Holiness
Today*, January 2002.

THE CULTURE OF INTERACTIVE HOLINESS

Karen Pearson and Tim Milburn

we arrived on campus as freshmen in the
early '80s. Under one arm we carried a box that
contained our "luxuries": a clock radio and a hot
pot. We connected with our world through a pay
phone down the hall. Twenty years later, we work
at a university where we relive that moving-in
experience each fall. Today the boxes have multi-
plied.

times have changed

This year we carried a television, VCR, microwave, fax machine, blender, CD player, cellular phone, computer, printer, refrigerator, stereo, two sets of speakers, and more—all for one student! Not necessarily luxuries, many of these tools are essential to the way today's students communicate and access information.

a new generation

Members of today's generation, beginning with those born in the early 1980s, live and operate in a changed world. The society in which they are growing up is unlike that of previous generations. Some of the changes are subtle, some extreme. To understand these young people, we must realize that their experiences, characteristics, and thoughts are shaped by the evolving world in which they live.

the need for interaction

Our students desire community, a place to belong. The broken family and our mobile society contribute to their need to connect to something meaningful. Young people have cell phones, beepers, multiple E-mail accounts, and call waiting; continuous interaction is their norm. Conversation and access to infinite information are big parts of their daily lives. They are at home in a culture that carries on an active dialogue with them. Theirs is not a passive generation that simply watches and absorbs television. The monitor they watch allows them to talk back and to control the flow of information.

a hunger for the spiritual

A desire to understand the spiritual and supernatural has intensified during this generation's coming of age. Memberships in Eastern religions transplanted in Western culture are on the rise. Stores are filled with literature, books, and music that seek to comfort our spiritual yearnings. The younger generations are the greatest consumers of these resources. They peruse the bookshelves and myriad web sites trying to find a place where faith actually makes sense.

living out holiness within the community

If we are to be the community that integrates the members of this generation into its fold, we must allow them to be active participants rather than casual spectators. We must begin a dialogue that capitalizes on their strengths, their ability to access and digest information.

We asked one of our own children, a member of this millennial generation, "What does holiness mean to you?" She answered, "Being clean with God." This sounds a lot like the last portion of 1 Thessalonians 5:23: "May your whole spirit, soul and body be kept blameless at the coming of our

Lord Jesus Christ." Let's not only ask the questions but also walk alongside our children in the discovery of what it means to be holy. Let's invite them to take an active role in discovering holiness.

The church must offer a community on a journey of discovery.

We also must help them belong. Our community, the church, must be a place that welcomes outsiders and celebrates diversity. We must offer a wide array of opportunities for young people to feel connected. They will begin to understand holiness only when they see it lived out through the community of faith and feel safe enough within that community to tackle the difficult issues and ask the hard questions—even if we don't have all the answers.

To this generation, the church must offer a community on a journey of discovery, one that seeks new ideas and allows people to experience God through their uniqueness as well as through their commonness. To be that kind of community, we have to be honest and authentic, doing all we can to build trust with this pivotal generation. As people of God, we must ask ourselves whether we communicate holiness in our lives, our churches, and our communities. And we must not shy away from the answer.

Karen Pearson serves as the director of residential life at Northwest Nazarene University. Tim Milburn serves as the director of campus life at Northwest Nazarene University. This article was first published in *Holiness Today*, January 2002.

HOLINESS: THE ONLY MESSAGE OF HOPE

teanna sunberg

i learned more about life than I taught about English in my downtown Kansas City junior high. Empty students came to class, and it was my mission to pour hope into every lesson and to reinforce it in every conversation. We studied careers and read about inspirational people. We wrote about our dreams and buried time capsules for our futures. The advantages of democracy, the doors that education opens, the stability and enjoyment of life that hard work brings—all were topics intended to plant seeds of hope.

Six years later and a world away from Kansas
City, I look from the sixth floor of a Soviet-era
apartment across a sea of crumbling rooftops,
and I find that these people, too, search for hope.
Across the Sofia skyline, the golden dome of an
Orthodox cathedral recalls hope from the halls of
tradition. The new Hilton promises hope in the
luxuries of capitalism. The palace of culture testi-
fies of hope drawn from what is praiseworthy in
the history of this Slavic land.

In Eastern Europe, hope is the promise of
democracy and the crown of freedom. Control
one's destiny and govern oneself, and today will
be better than yesterday.

Third-world countries embrace capitalism's
promises. Work hard to enjoy the material bene-
fits of wealth. Seek comfortable homes and stable
lives. Economic growth and stability will bring
hope.

America searches for her hope in education.
Educate the poor off the streets and the inmates
out of prison. Educate the young about AIDS.
Through the cleverness and ingenuity of humankind, every problem can be overcome and every
life enriched.

In every land and period of history, our dying
world seeks the hope for which humanity bar-
gains, begs, and battles but rarely finds. When
will we realize what hope is and is not? It does
not lie in the politics of democracy aiming to control the human hand. It will not be found in a sys-

tem of education that increases the capacity of the mind or in economic growth that fattens the wallet. Freedom, education, wealth—these are instruments to deliver what the heart desires. If the heart is evil, these instruments offer no hope to our dying world.

The message of real hope, authored by the Sculptor of humanity himself, is heart transformation.

The message of real hope, authored by the Sculptor of humanity himself, is heart transformation, because human desire and action originate from this core of our being. Whatever the heart desires, the hand will deliver, the mind will find, and money will provide. "For out of the overflow of the heart the mouth speaks," Jesus said (Matt. 12:34). He wanted us to understand that hope and salvation for our dying world flow only from hearts transformed by the love of Christ. This is the message that He taught, lived, and died to deliver.

To the political and religious establishment of Jesus' day, his message was scandalous and confrontational. Their laws forbade murder, but Jesus addressed the roots of hate in their souls. Their laws spoke against adultery, but He was concerned with the lust in their hearts. Their hands were clean. They were educated and economically stable men. But Jesus looked at their whitewashed exteriors and saw hearts full of dead men's bones.

To the searching voyagers who gathered on the stormy shores of life, to the weary souls who trudged up the steep mountainsides of their daily existence, Jesus offered real hope. They were diseased and full of evil spirits, and His touch healed them. They were hopeless, and His heart-transforming message changed them.

We of the Church of the Nazarene believe that God has raised us up for the specific purpose of proclaiming the message of heart transformation. It is called holiness. And it is the only message of hope for our world today. Jesus never meant for heart holiness to be a confusing sermon delivered from a pulpit or a theological term dissected in a seminary. He intended for us to deliver this message to the halls of our schools and the streets of our communities with hearts inwardly transformed and lives outwardly lived in holiness. He intended for us to change our world, one heart at a time.

Holiness is the only message of hope. Deliver it, and change our world.

Four years ago in my Moscow apartment, I received an E-mail message from a former student that sparked our correspondence throughout her high school years. Perhaps the seeds planted with essays and time capsules influenced Jakay's dreams for college and her future, but I pray she also reads Jesus' message of hope in my life and that it will change her heart.

This chapter is dedicated to all the JaKays in

our world: there is hope for your life, and it begins with your heart. And this article is dedicated to Nazarenes world wide: holiness is the only message of hope. Deliver it, and change our world.

Teanna Sunberg and her husband, Jay, serve as missionaries for the Church of the Nazarene in Sofia, Bulgaria. This article was first published in *Holiness Today*, April 2001.

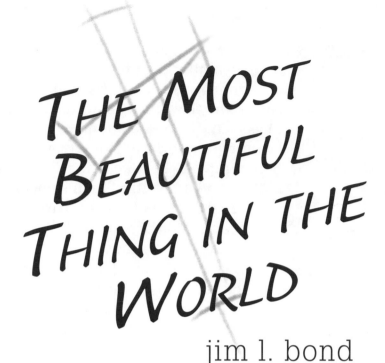

THE MOST BEAUTIFUL THING IN THE WORLD

jim l. bond

refreshing afternoon showers had come almost daily to the mountains above our home. Verdant beauty blossomed everywhere. Wildflowers danced in the soft summer breeze, resplendent whether standing regally apart or crowding merrily with countless others. The words of Henry Ward Beecher resonated within me: "Flowers are the sweetest things God ever made and forgot to give a soul." Imagine a flowerless world! How dull and drab! Thank God that He chose to adorn the landscape with the sublime grandeur of flowers.

> *There is nothing more beautiful than someone emulating the life of Jesus Christ.*

Is there anything in all creation more beautiful than flowers? Yes—unquestionably! As surely as God designed the flowers to beautify the earth physically, He created humankind to beautify the world spiritually through holy, righteous, godlike living! There is nothing more beautiful than someone emulating the life of Jesus Christ.

The intrusion of sin into the human situation forever tarnished our idyllic world. Evil's ugly moral blight has touched each of us: "We all, like sheep, have gone astray, each of us has turned to his own way" (Isa. 53:6). This is the basic problem of sin—our "own-way-ness." This selfish disposition has caused endless hatred, injustice, terrorism, war, and inhumanity. Our world situation is dreadful, monstrous, and ugly—clearly not the design of the Creator.

God's purpose for humankind is clear: "Be holy, because I am holy" (1 Pet. 1:16). To make this possible, God sent Jesus into our world to provide forgiveness for sin and a healing, cleansing remedy for our sinful, condition. Additionally, Jesus embodied holiness, thereby demonstrating how God intends us to live. What a contrast to our odious egocentricity!

Jesus lived a life of selfless love, a life of incomparable beauty and allure. We all are drawn to His compelling example: His love, humility, righteousness, meekness, justice, compassion, and gracious willingness to serve. It was said of Jesus that He "went around doing good" (Acts 10:38). He exemplified the positive qualities of the holy life. Holiness is about love, relationships, and investing oneself in others. It's the Jesus way, the way God intends us to live. "Be imitators of God . . . and live a life of love, just as Christ loved us" (Eph. 5:1-2).

To live such a life is humanly impossible, but what lies beyond our struggling reach becomes reality through the abundant grace of the God who commands us to be holy. William Temple described how this happens: "If you were to tell me to write a play like Hamlet or King Lear, I would tell you there is no way. Shakespeare could do it; I cannot. And if you were to tell me to live a life like Jesus, I would tell you there is no way. Jesus could do it; I cannot. But if the genius of Shakespeare could come and live in me, I could write plays like that. And if the Spirit of Jesus could come and live in me, then I could live like that." And that's exactly what God proposes to do in each of us!

The smallest flower is a divine work of art. But God creates His truest masterpiece when He takes sordid, sinful, and unsightly human lives, makes them holy and whole,

God creates His truest masterpiece when He takes sordid, sinful, and unsightly human lives, makes them holy and whole.

and transforms them into the likeness of Jesus Christ in ever-increasing glory (2 Cor. 3:18). There is nothing more beautiful in the entire world!

Jim L. Bond is a general superintendent in the Church of the Nazarene. This article was first published in *Holiness Today*, April 2002.

Our Pursuit of Holiness

john a. knight

sargent shriver, first director of the Peace
Corps, once delivered a chapel address at the University of Chicago to distinguished theologians,
philosophers, sociologists, historians, scientists,
and leaders of the laity. He quoted the Mexican
philosopher-historian Octavio Paz, who said, "The
sickness of the West is moral, rather than social
and economic. . . . The real, most *profound discord
lies in the soul of each of us*. The hedonism of the
West is the other face of its desperation; its nihilism ends in suicide, and in inferior forms of
credulity" (emphasis added).

Shriver then asked what could be done about
the world these haunting words describe. He answered his own question by saying, "I suggest we
commence the long hard task . . . of lifting ourselves from the 'pursuit of *happiness*,' to an addi-

tional and new level of . . . moral vigor; to 'the pursuit of *holiness'*" (emphasis added).

To all Wesleyans and Nazarenes, this challenge is compelling. Indeed, every true Christian believer possesses a serious desire to articulate an understanding of what this pursuit means and to experience it in his or her life.

God's holiness and love are always related. To be holy is to be like God.

Symbols of the Christian view of holiness are the antitheses of secular man's concepts of reality and value. Over against wealth is a life of simplicity; over against power is service; over against prestige is humility, and over against popularity is exaltation of Christ. These characteristics are a result of God's grace. They release into society a more-than-human energy, which transforms persons into new creatures in Christ and sets them on the road to moral and spiritual perfection—the pursuit of holiness.

The holiness we are to pursue is the holiness of God revealed in Jesus Christ. The word *holiness* describes the essential nature of God. To say that God is holy is to say that God is God. He is separate. He is different. "There is none like [him]" (Isa. 46:9). God alone is holy. Things, places, and persons become holy only because of their relation to the one holy God. Human beings are said to be holy when they are "set apart" for God's exclusive use. Holiness not only includes this vertical relationship to God but also a horizontal relationship with other persons and with the created order. Thus, God's holiness and love are always related. To be holy is to be like God.

In the New Testament, holiness is defined by Jesus Christ. Jesus is the "Holy One of God" (Mark 1:24, Luke 4:34, John 6:69). He is the embodiment of holiness. Man can become holy only by divine grace, not by good works or legalistic disciplines. John Wesley defined Christian holiness as "loving God with all the heart, soul, mind, and strength, and one's neighbor as oneself"—including one's enemies. It is the holiness demonstrated and embodied in the Person—life, death, and resurrection—of Christ. It is, in short, *Christlikeness.*

The biblical injunction to "follow peace with all men, and holiness" (Heb. 12:14, KJV) means to pursue holy living with all one's attention and strength. The word translated *follow* can also be translated *chase.* To follow holiness can never mean simply not to oppose it or to seek it half-heartedly. It must always mean to go after it will all zeal to possess. It is to desire it with such intensity that all other desires become as mere weak wishes in comparison.

The pursuit of holiness points to the significance of priorities. The priorities of the apostle Paul were upended by his encounter with the living Christ. He had failed to find peace with God through his own righteousness. But as Paul made his way to Damascus, Jesus Christ appeared to

him in a burst of surpassing glory, and he heard a
voice saying to him, "I have appeared to you *for
this purpose,* to make you a minister and a witness both of the things which you have seen and
of the things which I will yet reveal to you" (Acts
26:16, NKJV, emphasis added).

In that moment of conversion, the apostle began his pursuit of holiness—excellence of living
in Christ—and his values were transvalued. He
said, "What things were gain to me, these I have
counted loss for Christ" (Phil. 3:7, NKJV).

Paul was captured by a magnificent obsesson.
To the Philippians he wrote, "But one thing I do"
(3:13). Singleness of purpose, definite aims, proper priorities—these depict our pursuit of holiness.

With Paul we must wholeheartedly say, "I de-
termined not to know anything among you except
Jesus Christ and Him crucified" (1 Cor. 2:2, NKJV)
so "that I may know Him and the power of His
resurrection, and the fellowship of His sufferings" (Phil. 3:10, NKJV).

Pursuing holiness means continuously reor-
dering our priorities in obedience to the leadership of the Holy Spirit. In this way, we will be
what we are *in Christ,* do what we do best by *His
power,* and be all that we can be by *His grace.*

John A. Knight is a general superintendent emeritus in the
Church of the Nazarene. This article was first published in *Holiness Today*, April 2001.

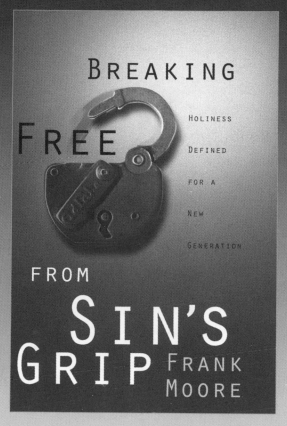